Raymond J. Curran

VNR VAN NOSTRAND REINHOLD COMPANY
NEW YORK CINCINNATI TORONTO LONDON MELBOURNE

Library of Congress Catalog Card Number: 82-8350
ISBN: 0-442-21208-9

Manufactured in the United States of America

Published by Van Nostrand Reinhold Company Inc.
135 West 50th Street, New York, N.Y. 10020

Van Nostrand Reinhold Publishing
1410 Birchmount Road
Scarborough, Ontario M1P 2E7, Canada

Van Nostrand Reinhold
480 Latrobe Street
Melbourne, Victoria 3000, Australia

Van Nostrand Reinhold Company Limited
Molly Millars Lane
Wokingham, Berkshire, England

15 14 13 12 11 10 9 8 7 6 5 4 3 2 1

Library of Congress Cataloging in Publication Data

Curran, Raymond J.
    Architecture and the urban experience.

    Includes bibliographical references and index.
    1. City planning.   2. Architecture—Environmental
aspects.   I. Title.
NA9050.08 1982   711'.4   82-8350
ISBN 0-442-21208-9   AACR2

Preface

As the limitations and shortcomings of the modern tradition in city building have become more apparent in recent years, a search for more meaningful criteria on which to base planning and design choices has become increasingly widespread. In essence, this search has largely focused on how to make cities less rigid and abstract, and on making them more supportive for people in their day-to-day experiences. In this search, many of the characteristics associated with historic cities, such as variety and complexity, as well as the greater sense of coherence that older urban forms provide, are replacing the more fragmented and impersonal characteristics associated with modern cities.

A central factor in this emerging trend concerns how people perceive, interpret, and use the public domain of the city. In order to be supportive of a wide variety of uses traditionally associated with urban life, the forms and spaces that constitute the public domain must be coordinated and based on an understanding of how they "speak" to people. Indeed, the city is perceived and interpreted as a kind of silent language. It expresses ideas that suggest and affect the way we use it on a day-to-day basis.

The aim of this book is to serve as a basic introduction for anyone interested and involved in the city-making process to the way the forms and spaces of the city can be expressive and supportive of the urban experience.

Rue Mouffetard, Paris

Contents

Figure 1-1. Ruins of Delos, Greece.

INTRODUCTION

In the many recent debates about the city, one point of agreement is becoming increasingly shared: that the true value of the city is not measured only in terms of its real estate, but also in terms of its *use value,* that is, in terms of how it affects people in their day-to-day experience.

Much of our daily experience of the city occurs within the collectively shared public spaces, or the public domain. Not only does the public domain provide for the most basic of the city's functions, access, but it also provides for and contains many other functions and activities synonymous with urban life. These have traditionally been organized, such as markets and public festivals, as well as spontaneous, including everything from the promenade and the meeting of friends to the appropriation of space for play, commerce, and display. While in the fine arts, painting, sculpture, etc., the "contents" embodied by the forms are generally symbolic and associated with abstract ideas, values, and feelings, in the built environment contents are essentially associated with use. When examining the experience of the city, therefore, it is necessary to consider the forms firstly and primarily in terms of their use value.

If we consider the ruins of the legendary city of Delos in Greece (Figure 1-2) or the remains of the Roman Forum (Figure 1-3), the forms and spaces we find are meaningful only insofar as we can associate them with the use they had. Together these tell us a great deal about the societies that lived in these cities. While the forms of the buildings tell us something about their contents as well as the esteem with which they were held, the spatial forms of the public domain tell us how people used the city and related to each other on a day-to-day basis. If we consider the modern example of a typical shopping development in the center of Pompano Beach, Florida (Figure 1-4), the form and use of the public domain, both in terms of access and other activities, also tells us a great deal about people and their interaction today.

Because *what* we build in terms of content generally involves major economic, political, and ideological challenges, matters of form, or *how* we build, and particularly as it affects the public domain, are often considered to be of secondary importance. Yet, as in Delos, Rome, and Pompano Beach, the form given to both buildings and public spaces also plays a large role in determining the quality and range of experiences that we have in our daily lives. As suggested, the content of the public domain involves much more than specific functions and activities. It involves a wide range and variety of more subtle and spontaneous uses that have always made urban life a very distinct and special experience.

Though the highly fragmented and linear process in which cities have been build in modern times remains largely intact today, changing values are

Figure 1-2. Ruins of Delos, Greece.

Figure 1-3. Ruins of the Roman Forum.

our experience of the city relies on the shared spaces of the public domain

increasingly demanding that a more holistic approach be developed. This reflects people's desire for a more complete and meaningful interrelationship with both the physical as well as the social context, and requires a high level of interdisciplinary understanding and cooperation between everyone involved in the city-making process. This is particularly important with regard to the production of a more meaningful and supportive public domain.

A central factor associated with the urban experience is how we perceive and interpret the visual forms that provide the physical context for the public domain. Though no simple, mechanistic, and predictable cause-and-effect relationship can be universally identified, how we perceive and interpret forms and spaces nevertheless strongly affects how we make use of the city. This is true with regard to both the primary function of the public domain, access, and the full range of other planned and spontaneous activities.

How we perceive the forms and spaces of the public domain as this relates to use is the subject of this book. Relying on an essentially descriptive approach, it is conceived as a basic introduction to the way forms and spaces act as sources of information and meaning and, in conjunction with planning choices, provides a supportive context for urban life. The aim is to provide anyone interested in the city and involved in the various aspects of the city-making process a better understanding of the language of visual forms and the way it can be utilized to better provide for people in their experience of the city.

Figure 1-4. Pompano Beach city center, Florida.

PART ONE

THE URBAN EXPERIENCE

A major part of the urban experience is the experience of the public domain. In addition to providing for a variety of ways to get from one place to another, the public domain provides many spaces for a wide range of additional functions and activities. Both planned and spontaneous, these uses, together with access, provide what can be described as the "glue" that bonds people together as well as all the individual parts that make up the city.

Facilitating access and a range of other uses, the public domain has historically provided perhaps the most accurate mirror of society as a collective enterprise. One might say that it is society writ large. Because of this, the character and quality of the public domain are necessarily key factors upon which our analysis of the urban experience must focus.

Part one provides a brief examination of how the public domain of the city in particular, functions as a container for access and other collective uses. The first section, "Cities, Form and Society; Changing Orders," provides a brief survey of the various approaches to the organization of urban form since the Middle Ages. Here, the nature of the public domain and the impact that various approaches to it can have upon our experience of the city are discussed. In section two, "The Architecture of Objects and the Decline of the Public Domain," basic characteristics of the Modern Tradition are examined. Section three, "Some Traditional Perspectives on the Urban Experience," looks at how the public domain has functioned in various historical situations, while section four, "Recent Developments and Current Trends," provides a brief survey of some of the more important characteristics of today's emerging tradition. Part one concludes with a general introduction to some of the basic factors that determine how we perceive and interpret the physical as well as the spatial forms that constitute the public domain of the city.

How we see and understand the city is a complex process. As mentioned in the introduction, the intention of this book is to provide a simple analytic process that is essentially descriptive in nature. It is not aimed, however, at providing any definitive descriptions of what forms mean to people nor of identifying how people actually use the city. Rather the more limited aim is to consider in general how forms gain meaning on one hand, and to examine in what ways this suggests ways in which people can use them.

Cities, Form and Society; Changing Orders

A society is an active organism, always in the process of becoming, always in the process of change. So are the forms it creates, which at once express and support this dynamic process. The forms that societies have produced in past eras can be seen as records of distinct value systems. This is particularly apparent when there have been dramatic changes in value systems and the associated forms.

Between the Middle Ages and the modern era, there have been three distinct approaches to the organization of the city. Referring to these as "orders" of organization, they have reflected changing value systems. In addition to expressing different modes of usage and different modes of human interaction, these orders also expressed different ways of relating to the natural environment.[1]

Of the three pre-modern orders, the earliest, the "closed" order, is associated with the medieval era. A small number of cities (and portions thereof) built within this order remain intact today. The second order, the "structured" order, is found in Renaissance cities and their derivatives, the baroque and neoclassic cities. Heavily influenced by earlier Greek and Roman concepts, this order provided organizational principles for many of the cities we live in today. The next order, the "pragmatic" order, is associated with the industrial era. This order is the basis of many cities in America. The most recent order, the "open" order, is associated with the modern era. In section two, this modern order will be examined in some detail.

Since most societies today are reevaluating the basic values that underlie modern life, pre-modern orders can be an invaluable source of comparison and learning. As we seek new forms of cohesion and try to reintegrate some of the values—perhaps too quickly dismissed in our rush to become modern—it is inevitable that new orders will be complex hybrids of both modern and pre-modern values and associated forms.

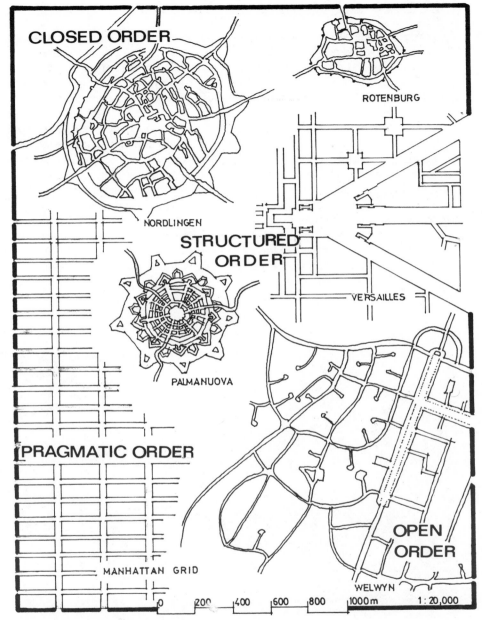

Figure 1-5. Four orders of urban development.

orders of organization reflect different value systems

5

THE CLOSED ORDER: 10TH TO 15TH CENTURIES

This order is generally characterized by a dense and apparently spontaneous disposition of buildings and an informal system of streets, squares, etc. Though lacking strict geometrical plans, the public domain of most medieval cities was nevertheless based on a well-organized system of access that was geared to access needs on a very local level, as well as to climatic and geographic conditions.

In typical examples of medieval cities (Figure 1-6 and 1-7), public spaces were small and intimate in scale, providing a strong sense of enclosure; thus our heading, "closed" order. The closed order was a very passive urban organization, geared to pedestrian use and small vehicles (pushcarts, horse-drawn wagons, etc.). As such, the tight public spaces, defined by highly homogeneous building forms, provided an urban context that was both expressive and supportive of a very intense public life. Entire communities functioned almost as single extended families, while the public domain provided a context that functioned as an active extension of an individual's private domain. It also acted as a strong bonding agent, both functionally and socially.[2]

Figure 1-7. Closed order development, San Giminiano, Italy.

the public domain was a strong bonding agent, social and functional

Figure 1-6. Closed order development, Colmar, France.

THE STRUCTURED ORDER: 15TH TO 18TH CENTURIES

From the fourteenth century on, major changes in the organization of cities paralleled the development of intercity trade and the rebirth (or renaissance) of classical concepts of order and thought. This was expressed not only in more easily negotiated systems of access, but in a much greater sense of clarity in the organization of the public domain in general. It is in this period that we find the reemergence of much earlier notions of geometry in the plans of cities.

These new systems, much larger and less intimate in scale, were geared to the more rapid movement of horse-drawn carriages as a principal mode of access. This facilitated movement through cities, which was unknown and irrelevant in the medieval era. It also expressed a new attitude about how people related to each other and to the larger natural context. Broad avenues and large squares, organized in highly structured plans, expressed, as in the example in Figures 1-8 and 1-9, both a greater control over nature and a desire for a greater sense of interaction with it.

The experience of such cities was at once uplifting and much less personal. Public spaces geared for movement and show often lacked the supportive intimacy of earlier eras.[3]

Figure 1-9. Structured order development, Washington D.C.

public spaces geared essentially for movement and show

Figure 1-8. Structured order development, Bath, England.

THE PRAGMATIC ORDER: 18TH AND 19TH CENTURIES

The industrial city was a direct product and expression of a system of values in which mass production was the dominant and almost exclusive concern. As such, industrial cities were often largely reduced to the most elementary and pragmatic level of repetitive building units, organized along essentially anonymous gridiron streets.

In sharp contrast to the closed and structured orders discussed previously, the typical city street, as in Figures 1-10 to 1-12, was essentially conceived for the sole purpose of providing access to workers' lodgings. In scale and character, such public spaces were otherwise generally unsupportive of other functions and activities. This became particularly problematic as the density of people and vehicles increased by the end of the nineteenth century.

Overcrowded, insalubrious, and lacking most of the qualities of earlier urban orders, it is from this urban order that the masses sought escape when public, and later private, transportation became available. This mass exodus continues to this day, particularly in American cities, though signs of a change are becoming increasingly apparent.[4]

Figure 1-11. Pragmatic order development, Oxford, England.

Figure 1-12. New Castle, England.

public spaces essentially conceived for access

Figure 1-10. Pragmatic order development, Brooklyn, N.Y.

THE OPEN ORDER: 20TH CENTURY

If cities mirror the societies that build them, it is clear that by the end of the nineteenth century the constraining rigidity of the industrial city was no longer perceived as an acceptable reflection. With the turn of the century, a new age dawned and with it came images that expressed the hopes and dreams of societies ready for change.

If the industrial city represents the thesis, the new open order represents the antithesis. From "garden" cities and suburbs to "radiant" cities and new towns, it has encapsulated a new freedom and a new life-style. A high level of mobility, personal isolation, and independence from a communal context—these are the chief characteristics of the new open order.[5]

While personal space and its real benefits were greatly increased, the advantages and supports of collective life, which cities had provided prior to the industrial period, faded from the popular memory of modern societies. Nuclear-family and car oriented, the open order has provided for the isolation of people and activities, as well as the buildings that contain them, and spread them out thinly on a wide and apparently limitless landscape (Figures 1-13 and 1-14).

Figure 1-14. Open order development, Connecticut suburb.

Figure 1-13. Open order development, Portsmouth, England.

the open order provides for the isolation of people, activities and the buildings which contain them

9

A basic characteristic of the modern approach to urban development has been the reduction of architecture to the status of self-referring and disengaged objects. The design of buildings no longer involves a cohesive exercise or, in the words of historian Sibyl Moholy Nagy, ''a syncretic vision of man in relationship to the social image of a community.''[5] At first based on nostalgia for self-sufficient farmhouses and the country cottages, the architecture of the Modern Tradition eventually became dominated by the technology and images of the mass-production process.[6]

Influenced by technological imagery and various movements in modern art, buildings in this new landscape have become increasingly conceived as machinelike artifacts and abstract sculpture, or as complex industrial megastructures. Other than the experience we have when looking at art objects, this modernistic environment has not addressed itself to our experience beyond the car and the private domain. Increasingly, the modern environment has become like a collection of isolated and unrelated fragments of every size and shape and only vaguely related to the human experience.

Figure 1-16. Sarcelle new town, France.

Figure 1-15. London suburb.

influenced by the imagery of modern technology

Figure 1-17. Creteil new town, France.

Figure 1-18. Office building, Zurich, Switzerland.

Figure 1-19. Office buildings, midtown Manhattan, New York.

buildings are conceived as mechanical artifacts

Figure 1-20. College buildings, Oxford University, England.

Figure 1-21. College building, University of Paris, France.

Figure 1-22. Office building, Stamford, Connecticut.

as pieces of abstract sculpture

or as complex megastructures

Figure 1-23. Le Miraille new town, Toulouse, France.

Figure 1-24. City center, Cumbernauld new town, Scotland.

Figure 1-25. Housing development, Brunswick Square, London.

Figure 1-26. City center, Indianapolis, Indiana.

Figure 1-27. City center, New Rochelle, New York.

Figure 1-28. Creteil new town development model, France.

like a collection of isolated and unrelated fragments

The Architecture of Objects and the Decline of the Public Domain

Directly related to the reduction of architectural structures to the status of objects, the most dominant characteristic of the modern tradition has been the deterioration and virtual disappearance of the public domain. No longer sustaining a range of activities traditionally associated with urban life, the public domain has been reduced to the exclusive use of the automobile, and the city, as a collection and system of spaces having multiple social as well as functional roles, was lost. This has paralleled the decline of public participation in government, industry, community affairs, etc., which represent the other vital dimensions of the public domain.[7] Accordingly, the city-making process has been fragmented into separate and specialized professions, including city and regional land-use planning, road and highway engineering, landscape architecture, architecture, etc. As in factory-line production, each is concerned with a single aspect of the process, while the effects of their input within the community has been lost to abstraction. Density, for example, is often a subject in its own right. It is discussed, not in terms of its impact on the actual physical context as people experience it, but in terms of abstract figures. Roads are no longer discussed in terms of how they relate to the communities they cut through, but in terms of traffic flows. Architecture, as we have seen, has become either the anonymous product of a quantitatively oriented production process or the personal expression of a designer and his client, detached and, often, almost defiant of the social and physical context beyond.[8]

Whether in new town situations, as in Creteil, France, or within existing urban situations, as in Boston (see Figures 1-28 to 1-30), buildings have been invariably conceived as isolated and unrelated structures. As for the spaces left between buildings, whether dedicated to the car and its storage or left for other uses, whether at ground level or on elevated decks and "streets in the sky," the overwhelming impression is that, in the haunting words of Gertrude Stein, "There's no there, there!"

Figure 1-29. Creteil new town, France.

Figure 1-30. Cambridge Street, Boston, Massachusettes.

roads are often considered in terms of traffic flows only

Figure 1-31. Manhattan's east-side F.D.R. Drive, New York City.

Figure 1-32. Brauchle-Ring, Munich, Germany.

Figure 1-33. Pompano Beach city center, Florida (opposite view 1-4).

Figure 1-34. Housing estate, Glasgow, Scotland.

Figure 1-35. La Grande Borne new town, France.

Figure 1-36. Housing estate, Liverpool, England.

Figure 1-37. Civic Square, Springfield, Massachusetts.

Figure 1-38. Charles Center, Baltimore, Maryland.

Figure 1-39. United Nations Plaza, New York City.

whether at ground level

or on elevated decks

Figure 1-40. La Defense office center, Paris, France.

Figure 1-41. Independence Plaza, Hartford, Connecticut.

Figure 1-42. World Trade Center Plaza, New York City.

Figure 1-43.

Figure 1-44.

Empire State Plaza, Albany, New York

Figure 1-45.

and streets in the sky

Thamesmead, new town, England

Figure 1-47.

Figure 1-46.

the overwhelming impression is that "when you get there, there's no there, there"

Figure 1-48. Suburban shopping center, Portland, Maine.

Figure 1-49. White Plains city center, New York.

Some Traditional Perspectives on the Urban Experience

Compared with the often claustrophobic characteristics of the closed order, the rigidity of the structured order, or the anonymity of the pragmatic order, the open order has unquestionably provided individuals with a degree of personal freedom and independence that cannot be underrated. It represents an advancement in our approach to the human development that will not be reversed. From a larger perspective, it can be noted that the trend toward greater individual freedom has been a major characteristic of the evolution of Western societies. Many of the real gains in self-development, as well as in science and technology, can be attributed to this particularly Western propensity. It is becoming increasingly evident, however, that this highly atomistic vision of the individual, vis-a-vis society and the physical environment in general, will require readjustment in the coming decades.[9]

Though of little concern in the early developmental phases of the modern era, it has become clear that both the health of our planet and of individuals who inhabit its surface require a degree of interdependency that Western societies have tended to underrate. While developing a more responsible attitude towards the natural elements is becoming an increasingly critical issue, the enormous emphasis on the individual, at the expense of basic social and convivial needs and responsibilities, appears increasingly to be a denial of human nature.[10] As Lewis Mumford suggested, "Our elaborate rituals of mechanization cannot take the place of the human dialogue, the dream, the living circle of mates and associates, the society of friends. These sustain the growth and reproduction of human culture, and without them the whole elaborate structure becomes meaningless—indeed actively hostile to the purposes of life." In the minds of people like E. F. Schumacher and Theodore Roszak, the agenda for the future must necessarily involve a reexamination and readjustment of the scales of involvement and the "levels of allegiance." In Roszak's words, this will require that institutions be "scaled down, slowed down, decentralized, and democratized."[10]

Figure 1-50. Venice, along the Grand Canal.

the collective experience of places where movement can be an end in itself

23

With regards to the city, and to the public domain in particular, we must limit our discussion concerning the balance between the individual and society to a brief survey of some of the ways the urban environment has provided for this through history. The public domain of the city has unquestionably been the most natural, flexible, and heterogeneous, as well as the most inclusive and permissive "institution" ever created by any society. At root, the urban experience is, and has always been, the collective experience of places and spaces conceived for linkage between people and for social interaction. It is the experience of places where movement can be an end in itself and in which you are always "where it's at." A spontaneous living theater, it's the experience of places where people come to see and to be seen, places to be a showman and for "doing your thing," places for relaxation and a change of pace, places for a sip or a snack, places for fairs and festivals, for rituals and celebrations, places for fun and games, places for establishing a sense of linkage and continuity with a cultural and historical tradition, places where shopping remains a joy and a creative social experience, the occasion for the meeting of friends and neighbors as well as strangers, places for the sharing of news and for the expression of views. The city is the close proximity of differences, the contrast of people and places as well as values and ideas.

Most of all, the city is for the young and the young at heart.

Figure 1-51. St. Aldate's Road, Oxford, England.

Figure 1-52. Tuilleries garden, Paris (photo by Fred Hersh).

Figure 1-53. Commonwealth Avenue, Boston, Massachusetts.

Figure 1-54. St. Malo (Britanny), France.

Figure 1-55. Brooklyn Bridge, New York City.

of places where you are always "where its at"

Figure 1-56. The Ramblas, Barcelona, Spain.

places where people come to see and to be seen

Figure 1-58. Rockefeller Plaza, New York City.

Figure 1-57. Djamaa Fna Square, Marrakech, Morocco.

Figure 1-59. Midtown Manhattan, New York City.

places for "doing your own thing"

Figure 1-60. Lincoln Center, New York City.

Figure 1-61. Champs Elysee, Paris.

Figure 1-62. Battery Park, New York City.

places for relaxation, a change of pace

Figure 1-63. The Promenade, Brooklyn Heights, New York City.

Figure 1-64. The Commons, Boston, Massachusetts.

Figure 1-65. Government Center Square, Boston, Massachusetts.

Figure 1-66. Aix-en-Provence, France (photo by Fred Hersh)

Figure 1-67. Battery Park, New York City.

and places for a sip or a snack

Figure 1-68. Guild Hall Square, Portsmouth, England.

Figure 1-69. St. Giles fair, Oxford, England.

Figure 1-70. Block party, New York City.

places for fairs and festivals, celebrations and rituals

Figure 1-71. Street fair, New York City.

and places for fun and games

Figure 1-72. Play area, Roosevelt Island, New York City.

Figure 1-73. Boulevard Jules Ferry, Paris.

Figure 1-74. Freiburg, Germany.

places for establishing a sense of continuity with the past

Figure 1-75. New College Lane, Oxford, England.

Figure 1-76. Karlstor Gate (Neuhauser Street), Munich, Germany.

its places where shopping remains a social experience

Figure 1-77. Rue Mouffetard, Paris.

for the meeting of friends and neighbors

Figure 1-78. Mahon, Minorca, Spain.

Figure 1-79. Market Square, Cirencester, England.

Figure 1-80. Harbor market, Helsinki, Finland.

its places for the sharing of news and the expression of views .

Figure 1-81. Place de la Bastille, Paris.

Figure 1-82. Barcelona, Spain.

the contrast of people and places, values and ideas

Figure 1-83. Midtown Manhattan, New York City (photo by Jerry Spearman).

Figure 1-84. St. Martin's canal, Paris.

Figure 1-85. West side piers, New York City (photo by Jerry Spearman).

the city is for the young and,

Figure 1-86. Mykonos, Greece.

Figure 1-87. New York City (photo by Jerry Spearman).

Figure 1-88. Washington Square, New York City.

Figure 1-89. Washington Square, New York City.

Recent Developments and Current Trends

It is a well-known fact that cities today and, to varying extents, throughout history, have been not only centers of exchange, production, fine arts, etc., but also places where many of the less attractive human instincts tend more naturally to surface. It is this perhaps more than the desire for space and personal freedom that led, both individuals and planners, to search for an alternative to the industrial city. People were searching for greater security and more control over their lives.[13] This search, together with a desire for greater personal space, mobility and freedom, as mentioned earlier, led to the development of the open order. In the open order, in spite of the real benefits it provides, one increasingly wonders whether one extreme has not replaced another. Indeed, many of those real qualities associated with earlier pre-modern (and preindustrial) cities seem to remain relevant to some of the basic human needs; variety and choice, human interaction and personal contact, creative participation, and a satisfying sense of belonging to a larger supportive context.[11] To what extent the traditional urban situations presented earlier are relevant today and can be incorporated into modern developments is becoming a major issue in today's city-making process. Many traditionally supportive characteristics are reemerging today as part of a trend towards a more people-oriented approach. The old dogmas of the Modern Movement are rapidly falling by the wayside. The bulldozer approach to urban renewal, for example, has largely been replaced by a more selective process, while community participation is becoming commonplace. New hybrids are emerging in which a more supportive combination of closed order and open order characteristics are providing a better balance and sense of cohesion without abandoning the real benefits of the modern tradition.

In terms of form, among the more typical characteristics familiar to everyone, the following can be noted: a new pride and respect for the urban heritage of the past through the conservation and restoration of old buildings, of entire streets and neighborhoods; a concern for local vernacular styles and building traditions and a greater desire to relate and "fit in" with existing settings; the revival of traditional building forms like the townhouse, and the reintroduction of low-rise buildings. It also includes the reemergence of distinct public spaces, both within existing cities and in new town and community developments.[16]

Figure 1-90. Venice cafe.

a more people-oriented approach

Figure 1-91. Colmar, France.

Figure 1-92. Quincy Market, Boston, Massachusetts.

Figure 1-93. Newport, Rhode Island.

Figure 1-94. Ghiradelli Square, San Francisco.

Figure 1-95. Chestnut Hill, Norwich, England.

a concern for local styles and traditions

Figure 1-96. Residential development, Le Marais, Paris.

Figure 1-97. Hillingdon civic center, London.

Figure 1-98. New vacation village, Minorca, Spain.

Figure 1-99. New shops Market Square, Whitney, England.

Figure 1-100. Parking garage, Heidelberg, Germany.

Figure 1-101. Residential development, Strasbourg, France.

the revival of traditional building forms

Figure 1-102. Residential development, Portsmouth, England.

Figure 1-103. Town houses, Philadelphia, Pennsylvania.

Figure 1-104. High-density, low-rise development, Anger, France.

Figure 1-105. Town houses, Bergues, France.

the reemergence of distinct public spaces, within existing cities

Figure 1-106. Paley Park, Manhattan, New York. (photo by Jerry Spearman)

Figure 1-107. Pompidou Center (Boubourg), Paris (photo by Fred Hersh).

Figure 1-108. Inner Harbor redevelopment, Baltimore, Maryland.

and in new towns and communities

In recent years, a reversion to a more holistic approach to urban development has begun to occur. Linking architectural and landscape design at an early stage within the planning process, a high degree of coordination makes it possible to avoid fragmentation and to provide distinct urban spaces for daily use.

In the three typical examples here, public spaces are clearly expressive and supportive of a range of activities and functions associated with urban life. The first example (Figures 1-109 to 1-112) is a mixed income community developed by the state of New York (through the Urban Development Corporation) on Roosevelt Island in New York city in the late sixties. Here a traditional city street, in parts arcaded, and a central square provide focal spaces for community life.

The second example, a residential community on the outskirts of Grenoble, France, was built for the Olympic games in 1968 (Figures 1-113, 1-114). While surrounded by athletic fields, playgrounds and parking areas, the development of this complex is organized around a series of interconnected plazas and pedestrian streets.

The third example is a good demonstration of the reuse and extension of older cities along waterfront areas in recent years. Built as a pier in San Francisco, this new commercial development is organized around distinct and well designed public spaces (Figures 1-115, 1-116). Like those at the neighboring Ghiradelli Square seen earlier (Figure 1-94), these have a character and quality of their own while being supportive of a variety of activities.

Figure 1-109.   View of Main Street.

Roosevelt Island, New York City

Figure 1-110.   View down central square.

Figure 1-111. A residential courtyard.

Figure 1-112. A view down Main Street.

Figure 1-113. Olympic Village.

*Olympic Village,
Grenoble, France*

Figure 1-114. View of a pedestrian street.

*Pier 39,San Francisco,
California*

Figure 1-115. Pier 39, San Francisco (looking North).

Figure 1-116. Pier 39, San Francisco (looking South).

Perception and the Visual Components of the Public Domain

Perception is such a basic aspect of our lives that we tend to take it for granted, as if it were neutral. Yet, what we see and how we interpret what we see is anything but neutral. What we see and how we interpret the visual environment involves many factors that are both innate in origin as well as acquired during a trial-and-error development process. The second aspect is heavily influenced by social and cultural conditions. With regards to both the innate and acquired influences, psychologists and physiologists are in general agreement that perception is highly selective and in part directed by basic drives.

Although the eyes are open "doors of perception," the mind does not actually "process" everything. One might say, the brain is "programmed" to seek out particular forms and patterns of visual stimuli that are relevant to human survival. This programming, which is more completely innate or instinctual in other animals, is also very different. A dragonfly, for example, having a different structure and associated needs, sees the world as a different place than what we humans see.[12]

As mentioned, many factors contribute to this programming in humans. The extent to which these are innate and operative from birth, or acquired and influenced by sociocultural factors, is a complex area of research that is increasingly providing useful insights. For the purposes of this book, we will borrow a few operative principles while turning our attention to an examination of our own personal experiences. We will seek to identify how and why particular physical characteristics suggest ways we can relate to and make use of the city. As mentioned earlier, we will not be looking for universal descriptions but rather for a better understanding of how subconscious processes by which the physical environment provides meaningful information operate. In short, we will examine our perceptual experience and try to "catch it in action."

THREE VISUAL COMPONENTS

As in scientific research, we cannot begin to analyze a complex phenomenon without to some extent structuring our approach and seeking a certain degree of detachment. Although our expectations invariably affect what we find, a more systematic approach to perception and analysis can nevertheless lead to a better understanding. Accordingly, our approach will consist in grouping the various visual elements that comprise the visual environment of the public domain under three basic headings or components. Each of these components provides an important source of information that our experience of the city relies on.

Our three visual components that make up the public domain and that we will be examining are outlined on the following page. They include: built and spatial forms, the treatment of defining surfaces, and ground treatment and furnishing. Although, as mentioned, these will be treated separately, there are aspects within each that invariably overlap and could equally be considered under different component headings (Figure 1-118). This overlap is one reason why a high level of coordination between the different professional groups involved in the city-making process is essential. The extent to which the different components are coordinated and provide consistent information is critical in our experience of the public domain. The lack of coordination between the visual components is frequently what lies at the root of the abstract and unsupportive urban conditions associated with many modern developments.

Figure 1-117. Photo by William Brooks III.

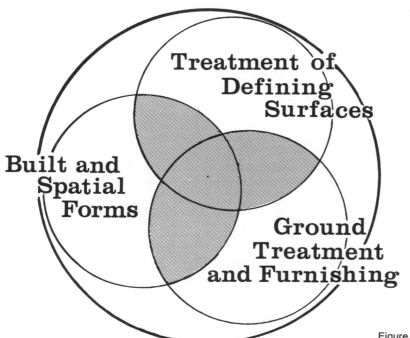

Figure 1-119. Henri Street Settlement Arts Center, New York City.

Component One: Built and Spatial Forms

Under Component One, our examination will focus on buildings and the exterior public spaces between them. We will consider how individual buildings, as forms, are expressive of their interior functions and also act as symbols for particular ideas and values.

Within the urban context, the expressive qualities of buildings extend beyond individual structures. Here one must consider not only the form of a building relative to other buildings, but also the role it plays in defining public spaces. Like built forms, the spatial forms of public spaces also convey essential information.

Figure 1-118.

Treatment of
Defining
Surfaces

Built and
Spatial
Forms

Ground
Treatment
and Furnishing

Figure 1-120. Stockholm (old city), Sweden.

Figure 1-121. Rome street market.

Component Two: The Treatment of Defining Surfaces

While the organization of facades can have an important impact on the scale and character of public spaces, the use of openings is also critical. Contributing to the scale and character of public spaces, windows and doors can be highly expressive of the uses contained within buildings. They also provide both visual and functional linkage between the exterior public domain and the interior private domain.

How this linkage occurs between these two domains, constitutes an important aspect of how we "read" and use the public domain.

Component Three: Gound Treatment and Furnishing

The third component will focus on the way the ground surface is treated in terms of materials, textures, patterns, etc., and on the various elements we put into our public spaces. This includes everything from monuments, which act as focal points, and trees, which fill up and subdivide spaces, to the use of bollards and seating.

As with components One and Two, the various visual factors included under Component Three can be highly expressive and supportive in our perception and use of the public domain.

Since many aspects of this third component are closely associated with land-use and activity choices, the interrelation between these is a vital consideration in the city-making process. This overlap is further discussed on the next page.

52

THE INTERRELATIONSHIP OF FORM AND CONTENT

Among the components of form that comprise the public domain, there is a great deal of overlap that occurs. Our visual experience of the public domain as a meaningful context relies on the consistency of the information that each of the components provides. As suggested in the introduction, however, when considering the use value of the city, perhaps the most important overlap to be considered is that between the three components of form and land-use planning, which largely determines the basic functions and activities one finds in the public domain. Contrary to what is often believed, the use of public spaces cannot be described as a design problem alone, nor, conversely, can land-use choices occur without the support of a physical context.

As opposed to painting and sculpture, in which the content of forms consist mainly of abstractions (feelings, memories, etc.), the contents of form in the city's public domain is associated primarily with use and use ideas.

The areas of overlap between form and land-use planning, where the public domain is concerned, can be depicted as in Figure 1-122.

Although building forms are largely determined by the type of uses they contain (which again is a form/content relationship), as well as building technology and density, the street plan, which is determined by the access systems chosen, is also a critical form determinant.

The introduction of superblocks, for example, has often meant that buildings could be set back from the street, thereby eliminating them as defining elements for the public domain. With regards to the choice of access systems, which determine street plans, again there is a major overlap. This affects not only the range of uses possible within the public domain but, together with zoning controls affecting building densities building height, and building lines, affects the spatial form of public spaces. As such, an almost complete overlap occurs between planning choices affecting content with Component Three. Of our three components, only Component Two remains relatively independent of planning choices, as it directly concerns the public domain.

When considering many of the examples of urban developments that are a product of the Modern Tradition, it becomes clear that many of the shortcomings discussed earlier, in terms of the expressive and supportive qualities associated with use, can be ascribed to a lack of sufficient overlap between the two spheres of form and land-use planning.

The form of buildings is often dealt with independently by architects so that the coordination required to produce public spaces is lacking. The results, as in many of the examples seen earlier, is a collection of abstract forms surrounded with meaningless spaces that are neither public nor effectively private. Rather, they are often useless no-man's zones. Similar limitations can be seen with regard to the treatment of public spaces, which are often left as

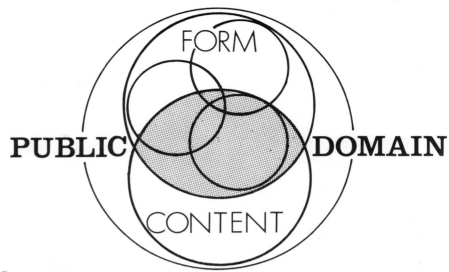

Figure 1-122

afterthoughts and with which the landscape architect is expected to perform minor miracles.

One of the objectives of the discussion that follows in Part Two is to underline the fundamental necessity of eliminating the senseless divisions between the various professional groups dealing with the city and to emphasize the importance of the basic relationship between form and content. If the experience of the city, and the expressive and supportive qualities upon which it relies, is to be reinstated into and made a focus of the city-making process, the linear process of the modern tradition must be replaced by a truly holistic one. In such an approach, human criteria, associated with human experience, must become fundamental.

Notes and References—PART ONE

1. In her book *The Matrix of Man* (Praeger, New York, 1968, p. 158) Sybil Moholy Nagy proposed that cities throughout history have been based on three archetypal and recurrent organizational principles: geomorphic, concentric, and orthogonal. Her examination suggests that there is a relationship between these and the norms which govern the societies creating them: "The geomorphic approach is organic, characterized by interrelated growth between landscape and building; the concentric approach is ideological, deriving from a commitment to a supramundane ideal; the orthogonal concept is pragmatic, adjusting the city to constantly changing requirements of communication and expansion." Our three orders suggested here roughly correspond to these three systems although the grid-iron of the Industrial period, the 'pragmatic order,' is only one very rigid version of the orthogonal system. Precedents of this order can be found among the earliest cities in history.

2. In *Town and Square: From the Agora to Village Green* (Columbia University Press, New York, 1959), Paul Zucker suggests that during the medieval era when cities grew by and large by accretion, the organization of the city as a total system was neither understood nor of particular concern; "only at the end of the Middle Ages did the town become the symbol of any political or social idea." (p. 97) Nevertheless, as Lewis Mumford argues in *The City in History* (Harcourt, Brace, and World, Inc., New York, 1961), though the medieval city, as a product of "organic planning," does not begin with a preconceived goal, the final product, as in the case of Sienna, is "hardly less unified than a preformed geometric pattern." (p. 302) The conception of space however is seen by both historians as an unconscious concern, although protection from the elements must have been one conscious determinant. "The very narrowness of medieval streets made their outdoor activities more comfortable in winter." (Mumford)

3. Both the organization of plans and the design of public spaces in this period reflected a conscious desire to make the city a reflection of a controlled social order and a place for public participation. The large scale application of these development principles towards the end of this era, however, paralleled a deterioration of the public domain as a context for active social interaction. Increasingly, public spaces, and squares in particular, became places for movement and show rather than for gathering. In his book, *The Fall of Public Man* (New York: Vintage Books, 1978), Richard Sennett suggests that in the early 18th century, the square as a 'free zone' was replaced by large symbolic spaces "no longer designed with a lingering, congregating crowd in mind." (p. 54) While a variety of activities in spaces like Place Vendome in Paris were forbidden, the new squares of London were in fact semiprivate parks, accessible to surrounding land-owners only.

4. The use of grid-iron plans and anonymous highly repetitive streets divested the city of its more complex social role. It is in this context that Richard Sennett in the aforementioned book argues that man the actor and maker was replaced by man the silent and passive observer. As such, the public domain became divested of its historical role as a place for active human interaction. It is in response to such conditions that most utopian ideas and ultimately the notion of garden cities, as conceived by reformers like Ebenezer Howard in his influential book *Garden Cities of Tomorrow* (MIT Press, Cambridge, 1965, original publication 1898), were developed.

5. Some of the earliest ideas for the modern city were associated with the Futurist movement as provided by Antonio Sant'Elia and Filippo Mannetti. In the Manifesto of Futurist Architecture, provided at an exhibition in Milan in 1914, Sant'Elia proclaimed that "we must invent and rebuild the Futurist city; it must be like an immense, tumultuous, lively, noble work site, dynamic in all its parts; and the Futurist house must be like an enormous machine." The later development of these principles by the CIAM group were summarized by Le Corbusier in his *Charter of Athens* in 1941. One of these stated that, "the keys to town planning are to be found in the four functions: housing, work, recreation, and traffic."

6. The relationship of architecture to the public domain as suggested in the quotation by Sybil Moholy Nagy *(Landscape, Winter 1966–67)* was rejected by the Futurist as well as all the later derivative movements (CIAM, Bauhaus, etc.). The relationship of this with the changes in capitalism are discussed by Manfredo Tafuri in his book *Architecture and Utopia, Design and Capitalist Development* (MIT Press, Cambridge, 1980). With regards to the present crisis of modern architecture, he suggests that a meaningful change cannot occur within the confines of the limited position which design is in today. He suggests that the crisis is one "of the ideological functions of architecture." He further suggests that "the search for an alternative within the structures that condition the very character of architectural design is indeed an obvious contradiction of terms." (p. 181)

7. The notion of the public domain as encompassing every aspect of collective life and not just the exterior public spaces is a critical distinction here. One of the more influential discussions of this larger concept of the public domain is Hannah Arendt's *The Human Condition* (University of Chicago Press, 1958). Of particular interest is her emphasis on the notion of collective and creative action as the basis of city life. "The polis, properly speaking, is not the city-state in its physical location, it is the organization of the people as it arises out of acting and speaking together, and its true space lies between people living together for this purpose, no matter where they happen to be." (p. 198) With regards to the public domain as a physical environment, she suggests that "the public realm, as the common world, gathers us together and yet prevents our falling over each other, so to speak. What makes mass society so difficult to bear is not the number of people involved, or at least not primarily, but rather that the world between them has lost its power to gather them together, to relate and to separate them." (p. 53)

8. In this connection, and referring back to the opening statement in the introduction, the emphasis on buildings as objects has tended to focus their value in terms of exchange rather than use. This notion of exchange as opposed to use value, and particularly as this affects the public domain, has been discussed by many sociologists, including Henry Lefebvre in his classic *Everyday Life in the Modern World* (English translation, Harper Torchbooks, New York, 1971) as well as the later untranslated books *Le droit a la ville* and *Espace et politique*.

9. This critical aspect of human nature has been emphasized in the work of many psychologists in recent years. Of particular interest is the work of Ernest Becker who in *The Birth and Death of Meaning* (The Free Press, New York, 1962) and *The Denial of Death* (The Free Press, New York, 1973) has examined the importance of social support systems in providing the individual with a sense of meaning and stability. "What characterizes modern life is the failure of all traditional immortality ideologies to absorb and quicken man's hunger for self-perpetuation and heroism." Becker maintains that "the most terrifying burden of the creature is to be isolated, which is what happens in individuation". (Denial, p. 171) This problem of the fragmentation of the modern psyche is something which has been a dominant theme in both modern philosophy from Kierkegaard to Sartre as well as modern literature.

10. The Lewis Mumford quotation is from his book *The City in History,* and the references to Roszak are from a PBS television interview (Bill Moyer's Journal, 1981). Book references for Roszak and Schumacher are provided below.

11. In another influential book, *The Uses of Disorder* (Penguin Press, London, 1970), the sociologist Richard Sennett, referring to the classic *Democracy in America* by Alexis de Toqueville (first published in 1835), considers some of the social causes which led to the development of oversimplified modern developments and suburbia in particular. In his analysis,

he suggests that "in the name of avoiding painful confusion, of establishing the 'decencies' of life as regnant, the scope of human variety and freedom of expression is drastically restricted." This is particularly problematic with regards to young people as they enter the teenage period. In her book *With Man in Mind* (MIT Press, Cambridge, 1970), Constance Perin suggests that "juvenile delinquency occurs everywhere, but in the suburbs especially the entire question of teenagers' behavioral expectations and the lack of resources with which to meet them is an issue yet to be faced by public policy." (p. 153)

12. The mechanisms of perception and the processes through which the human mind derives meaning from the world remain perhaps the last and most challenging frontier. A large amount of work is being done in this area today. A good introduction to some of this research, first presented by the BBC in *1976 Reith Lectures in England* is Colin Blakemore's *Mechanics of the Mind* (Cambridge University Press, 1977). Another good introduction is *The Psychology of Consciousness* by Robert Ornstein (Penguin Books, New York, 1975). In specific connection with questions of the built environment, perhaps the best summary available on research is Amos Rappoport's *Human Aspects of Urban Form* (Pergamon Press, 1977).

ADDITIONAL RELATED REFERENCES (PART ONE)

Allsopp, Bruce. *The Study of Architectural History*. Studio Vista, London, 1970.

Ardrey, Robert. *The Territorial Imperative*. Fontana / Collins, Glasgow, 1967.

Bell, Colin and Colin, Rose. *City Fathers, The Early History of Town Planning in Britain*. Praeger, New York. 1969.

Benevolo, Leonardo. *Aux sources de l'urbanism modern*. Horizons de France, Paris, 1972.

Blowers, Andrew and Hammett, Chris, and Sarre, Philip (eds). *The Future of Cities*. Hutchinson Educational, London, 1974.

Cooper, David. *The Death of the Family*. Penguin Books, New York, 1971.

Evenson, Norma. *Paris: A Century of Change, 1878–1978*. Yale University Press, New Haven, 1979.

Farbstein, Jay and Kantrowitz, Min. *People in Spaces*. Prentice Hall, New Jersey, 1978.

Goodman, Robert. *After the Planners*. Penguin Books, New York, 1972.

Huizinga, John. *Homo Ludens, a study of the play element in culture*. The Beacon Press, Boston, 1955.

Jacobs, Jane. *The Death and Life of Great American Cities*. Vintage Books, New York, 1961.

Kopp, Anatole. *Town & Revolution, Soviet Architecture and City Planning 1917–1935*. George Braziller, New York, 1970.

Lefebvre, Henri. *Le droit a la ville*. Editions Anthropos, Paris, 1968.

———. *Espace et politique*. Editions Anthropes, Paris, 1968.

Morris, A. E. J. *History of Urban Form, Prehistory to the Renaissance*. George Goodwin Ltd., London, 1972.

Mumford, Lewis. *The Urban Prospect*. Harcourt Brace Jovanovich, New York, 1956.

Pirenne, Henri. *Medieval Cities, Their Origins and the Revival of Trade*. Princeton University Press, 1969.

Poete, Marcel. *Introduction a l'urbanisme*. Editions Anthropos, Paris, 1967.

Raban, Jonathan. *Soft City*. Fontana / Collins, Glasgow, 1974.

Rifkind, Carole. *Main Street, The Face of Urban America*. Harper Colophon Books, New York, 1977.

Roberts, Robert. *The Classic Slum*. Penguin Books, New York, 1974.

Roszak, Theodore. *The Making of a Counter Culture*, Faber and Faber, London.

———. *Unfinished Animal*. Faber and Faber, London, 1975.

Rudolfsky, Bernard. *Streets for People*. Doubleday, New York, 1969.

Schumacher, E. F. *Small is Beautiful*. Harper & Row, New York, 1973.

———. *A Guide for the Perplexed*. Harper Colophon Books, New York, 1977.

Slater, Philip. *The Pursuit of Loneliness*. Penguin Books, New York, 1970.

White, Morton and Lucia. *The Intellectual Versus theCity*. Oxford University Press, 1962.

Willis, F. Roy. *Western Civilization, An Urban Perspective*. D. C. Heath and Co., Lexington, Mass., 1973.

Zijderveld, Anton C. *The Abstract Society, A Cultural Analysis of Our Time*. Penguin Books, New York, 1970.

PART TWO

THE VISUAL COMPONENTS
OF THE PUBLIC DOMAIN

In addition to the greater density and variety of people and activities, the experience of the urban environment, as opposed to the experience of the suburban or rural environments, is unique by virtue of the character and quality of the public domain. Whereas the public domain provides a system of access wherever humans live, in the urban context, the public domain, as suggested at the start of Part One, has historically, and in its various "orders" of organization, provided two uniquely urban qualities. The first concerns the range of access modes facilitated, and the second concerns the range of other functions and activities that are also facilitated there.

The basic underlying motivation and raison d'etre for city-making throughout history, that of maximizing access between individuals and their activities, relies on the expressive and supportive qualities of the public domain. Where access is uniquely associated with mechanized and wheeled vehicles, as has been largely the case in modern developments, access is essentially a road engineering and planning question. When considering a wider range of access modes, however, the rules of the game, unchanged throughout history, revert back to the laws that govern that most complex and enigmatic of all mechanisms, the human creature. The extent of access needed and desired by humans today notwithstanding, the fact remains that where it is sought beyond what the car can provide, the expressive and supportive qualities of the public domain in which access occurs becomes a basic factor.

The second uniquely urban quality that distinguishes the urban public domain and partially depicted in the photos in section three of Part One, concerns all of those countless activities that occur within the urban public domain other than, but often associated with, access.

In Part Two, our examination of the visual experience of the public domain will consider how each of the three components outlined at the end of Part One operate as sources of information. As suggested, our concern will be with both the expressive qualities of forms as well as with their supportive qualities. In other words, we will be concerned with how the visual components of the public domain facilitate use, both in terms of access and other functions and activities.

COMPONENT ONE
BUILT AND SPATIAL FORMS

In our examination of the experience of the public domain, the first and most important elements that concern us are the buildings. The forms of buildings, determined by their shapes and sizes, can be highly expressive and a vital source of information in our understanding and use of the city. To a varying extent, the forms of buildings tell us about their contents. Of equal importance, when buildings are placed together, the relationships they have in terms of the shapes and sizes of their forms as well as the patterns they produce in space, are also sources of information.

Within the context of the city, when buildings are percieved as surfaces defining distinct spaces, their expressive qualities are associated not only with uses they contain "inside," but also with uses they contain "outside." The spatial forms of public spaces, like the spaces inside buildings, are also expressive of their functions.

It is the interrelationship of built and spatial forms, as in the example of Florence (Figure 2-1), which provides the basic expressive and supportive context of the city and of the urban experience.

Figure 2-1. Florence, central city.

built and spatial forms provide the basic context for the urban experience

THE EXPRESSIVE QUALITIES OF BUILT FORMS

The meaning the physical environment has for us, as discussed in Part One, is based on a complex interrelationship of innate factors and acquired knowledge. Without delving into these areas of research, in our essentially descriptive approach here, we can broadly distinguish two general sources of meaning in our experience of the physical environment. The first is basically associated with our own physical nature and makeup. Though the understanding we derive from this source is at least in part developed through our experience with the world, we can describe it as an innate source of meaning. The second source of meaning we will consider is more specifically developed through our experience and is heavily influenced by our social and cultural context. We can describe it as an acquired source of meaning. As mentioned, however, these two sources of meaning are heavily interrelated.

With regards to the first, the more essentially innate source of meaning, two useful references will be relevant in our discussion. The first is Geoffrey Scott's classic, *The Architecture of Humanism,* and the second, a more recent work, is Rudulf Arnheim's *The Dynamics of Architectural Form.*[1] In principle, both of these references suggest that our understanding of and reaction to architectural (and spatial) forms is based on our tendency to "transcribe architecture into terms of ourselves." This includes human movement, moods, response to gravity, etc. Based on these, it is the ideas forms produce that become the basis of our reactions. Thus, as Scott has suggested, when we see a top-heavy building, it produces ideas of instability, while an ill-proportioned room (like one much too low for its size) produces ideas of restriction. Along an essentially similar line of thinking, Arnheim has suggested that we interpret forms as "visual analogies" to their practical functions. In other words, forms are meaningful to us as expressions of functions they perform. Thus we interpret forms in action or dynamic terms.

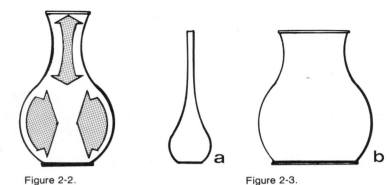

Figure 2-2. Figure 2-3.

Arnheim's example of Greek vases is a particularly useful one in that, as we will see later, the basic functions of the vase, containing and dispensing, closely parallel the functions of the public domain. The two shapes that comprise the overall form of the vase are the bowl and the neck. The bowl is a convex form, which, in Arnheim's words, "gathers the contents of the vessel around the center." Arnheim further suggests that "roundness as a visual dynamic quality expresses containing." The long tubular form of the neck of the vase, in contrast to the bowl, is expressive as a visual analogy of the function of dispensing and of movement. (Figure 2-2)

Variations in the size and length of the neck will dispense differently as well as be expressive of these differences. Thus, in Figure 2-3, thin neck (a) will dispense more slowly and precisely than a wide neck (b). Similar differences would occur with variations in the shape of the bowl. While a small and delicate bowl might be appropriate for perfume, a large heavy bowl would be suited for water.

forms are interpreted as "visual analogies" for the functions they perform

As suggested, it is not form in itself that provides a source of meaning in our interpretation. Rather it is the function the form is seen to "perform" and the clarity with which this is suggested that provides us with meaningful information.

Turning to another type of utilitarian device, like a bridge, again we find that the function is expressed in the form as an analogy to the action it performs. In the example of the classic Firth of Forth Bridge in Scotland (Figure 2-4), the form seems literally to be "leaping" across the river while carrying a perfectly horizontal line of movement through its structure, a railroad track. As Geoffrey Scott has suggested, form "has stirred our physical memory," which is in part based on a very personal awareness of the forces of gravity. The grace with which this structure performs its function, as it defies the forces of gravity, is what provides the expressive quality it has.

The expressive quality of architectural forms is particularly evident in buildings where the function is simple and differentiated. This can be seen in the example of a football stadium, as in the example on the outskirts of Milan in Figure 2-5. Here the "bowl" is very clearly a visual analogy of the containing function of the building.

Figure 2-5. Sports stadium, Milan, Italy.

Figure 2-4. Firth of Forth Bridge, Scotland.

Figure 2-6. Church Gorham, Maine.

The expressive quality of forms in more functionally complex buildings can also be found to varying degrees. In the example of a traditional church, as in Figure 2-6, the basic form of the main building, with its four containing surfaces and pitched roof, like the bowl of a vase, provides an elementary expression of containment. More specific indications of the uses contained relies on the relationship of the interior space (or spaces) of the building to the exterior context, as expressed through the various openings in the containing surfaces (Component Two).

Figure 2-7. Guggenheim Museum, New York City.

The form of the tower is visually associated with the idea of "standing up" against the forces of gravity. In Scott's words, "A spire, when well designed, appears as common language testifies—to soar." He further suggests that "we identify ourselves, not with its actual downward pressure, but its apparent upward impulse." As such the tower has historically been associated with man's power and defiance of the forces of gravity as well as his reach toward a higher reality.

The distinction between differentiated and more generalized expressions of containment is evident in Frank Lloyd Wright's Guggenheim Museum in New York (Figure 2-7). While more generalized administrative functions occur within cubistic forms, the major exhibit space is contained in a distinct bowllike form.

The notion of forms as containers for types of activities—creating form typologies—has historically been an essential source of information in our understanding of cities. In the typical example, in New York City (Figure 2-8), the apartment as a form typology plays an important role in the legibility of the city. In this case, a church steeple differentiates one of these forms and provides a landmark.

In conjunction with the last example, we can now briefly consider our second source of meaning with regards to built forms: symbolism. In essence, this originates not necessarily in the functional expressive qualities of forms, but rather in the societies that create them.

In the first, more intrinsic source of meaning, as we have seen, forms act as indications or signs of their functions. Symbolism, as a source of meaning, derives from the fact that all that we do as members of a social group is, in effect, a form of communication. Gestures, clothes, the things we build—all act as languages as a result of the ideas that become associated with them.[2]

With regards to architecture, Arnheim suggests that "symbolism begins to come into play when a building's design uses shapes that carry a conventional meaning." Thus, forms, in addition to being expressive as signs of their functions, also are expressive because of ideas and values that come to be associated with them. These associations may or may not have any direct relationship with function. In our example of the church, the tower has become a symbolic expression of culturally shared metaphysical values.

In the case of the castle as a typology, the forms that comprise this structure are expressive of specific functions. Though basically similar to our church house and tower, like the variations in Greek vases discussed earlier, differences in the two composite forms express different functions. In addition, however, these specific variations have become expressive of specific ideas derived from and associated with the original functions. In the example in Figure 2-10, borrowing all the historic conventions, this casle was built as a summer house. Though lacking any of the functions that originally generated this form, the ideas of strength, exclusion, independence, etc., have been retained.

Figure 2-8. Greenwich Village, New York City.

forms act as signs of their functions

Figure 2-9. Blarney Castle, Ireland.

Figure 2-10. Anif Castle, Salzburg, Switzerland.

forms act as symbols

63

Figure 2-11. Goetheanum Institute residence, Dornach, Switzerland.

In the example of a house at the Goetheanum Institute in Dornach, Switzerland (Figure 2-11), the basic typology of a residential building, the traditional house, has been retained. In spite of the highly unorthodox treatment, expressive of specific ideas known to the members of this institution, the basic conventions associated with houses make its function apparent to everyone.

In Figure 2-12, an entrance pavillion in Barcelona's Parque Guell, by Antonio Gaudi, relies again on the basic forms of the container and tower. In sharp contrast to our castle, however, or to the church discussed earlier, the specific shapes and treatment of these two forms provides a whole different set of associated or symbolic references. The gingerbread quality provided by Gaudi makes clear references to the Western tradition of the fairy tale. As such it suggests a playlike quality that is consistent with the overall intentions for the park. We will return to the question of building treatment under Component Two.

An important characteristic of symbolism in forms is that it generally operates as part of a system of meaning and according to specific rules. Though specific forms, like specific words, become symbols associated with ideas, values, institutions, etc., their meaning also relies on how they relate to other forms.

Figure 2-12. Entrance pavillion, Parque Guell, Barcelona, Spain.

by association with ideas

64

The concept of a color, like brown, for example, is only really meaningful when considered as a distinct part of a spectrum of colors. The same is true of building forms. If all buildings had (similar) towers, no symbolic ideas or values could be associated with its use. A church communicates specific ideas through its tower, not only because of its specific detailing as we have seen, but because, in general, other buildings don't have towers. It is in this sense that the physical forms we build can act, when conceived within the context of established associations, as a language through which communication occurs.

In the examples of cities in New England (Figure 2-14) and on a Greek island (Figure 2-13) our understanding of the forms relies on both the sign quality of the buildings as well as the symbolic associations they have. While the first source of meaning, as we have seen, is more intuitive in nature, the second is essentially cultural.

Figure 2-14. Lewiston, Maine.

Figure 2-13. Santorini, Greece.

as part of a "system" of ideas

65

The Confusion of Meaning in Architectural Forms

Both the more intuitive functional as well as the symbolic expressive qualities of built forms are essential sources of meaning in our understanding and use of the city. When these semantic qualities are disregarded in the city-making process, the result is often confusing. Cities become abstract and irrelevant to the people trying to use them. A reliance on written signs, maps, etc., becomes increasingly essential as interpretive devices because forms no longer "say" what they mean or mean what they say.

Early examples of this confusion in both the functional and symbolic qualities of forms began to occur in the early decades of this century. As with the castle summer house in Salzburg discussed earlier, the arbitrary use of forms became increasingly common. The house in a Paris suburb (Figure 2-15), for example, uses forms that are functionally and symbolically irrelevant to the building's actual use.

Within the modern era, the development of an aesthetics of high technology, starting with the Bauhaus and the "International Style," although often associated with new functions like office buildings and factories, soon became a source of semantic confusion. Increasingly applied to all types of buildings, the notion of typology as a vital source of information in our reading of the built environment became diffused and eventually lost. One could no longer determine whether a building was a hospital, an office building or a residential block. It is a similar devaluation of semantic codes as that which occurred when the classical style of architecture became universally applied by the end of the nineteenth century. It subsequently became universally meaningless since one could no longer tell the difference between a church or a bank, theater, etc.[3]

Although, as with any language, new ideas, values and functions produce constant changes in the forms we use, it seems increasingly apparent that designers, if they are to build forms perceived as meaningful by the general public, they must to some extent acknowledge the existing system of associations in any given situation. The built environment, after all, is not primarily meant to impress people but rather to serve as a context in which people can live their lives on a day-to-day basis.

Figure 2-15. Private house, Clamart, France.

when semantic qualities are disregarded the result is often confusing

THE EXPRESSIVE AND SUPPORTIVE QUALITIES OF BUILDING RELATIONSHIPS AND SPATIAL FORMS

Beyond the expressive qualities of individual buildings, the way they are disposed and related to each other provides another vital source of information. As with the relationshp of surfaces that produces built forms, the relationship of buildings in space is also expressive of functional ideas.

Research in various schools of psychology has indicated that particular relationships or patterns of stimula are generally perceived as meaningful, presumably because they are relevant to our survival. Other creatures, like our dragonfly, perceive other patterns that are relevant to their survival. Three basic patterns we tend to fix on are associated with the laws of proximity, continuity, and closure (Figure 2-16). In general, what these laws indicate is that we tend to perceive (and seek) these relationships rather than independent elements.[4]

With regards to building relationships, beyond general grouping associated with proximity, we can identify two basic patterns that are relevant in our experience of the city: linear patterns and cluster patterns. These are associated with the laws of continuity and law of closure mentioned above.

In our examination of the expressive and supportive qualities of the public domain, these two basic relationships are of immediate relevance. With a close parallel to the two composite forms of our vase, the neck and the bowl, these two patterns are expressive by analogy to the functions they suggest and perform. The linear pattern, like the neck of the vase, is expressive of the function of movement, which it suggests and facilitates.

In Figure 2-17, a street in the old New England town of Bath, Maine, the linear pattern of the individual houses is clearly expressive of the linking and access function of the public domain.

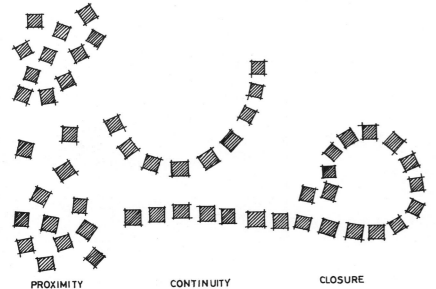

PROXIMITY   CONTINUITY   CLOSURE

Figure 2-16. Three basic gestalt relationships.

Figure 2-17. Bath, Maine.

The cluster pattern, like the bowl of the vase, is expressive of the function of containing. Here, the surfaces are related so as to focus attention and usage within a distinct location. In the example of an elephant house in the London Zoo (Figure 2-18), we can see that, beyond the proximity of the individual elephant pavilions, a distinct cluster pattern has been produced.

Within these two basic patterns, the use of building relationships to produce exterior conditions supportive of various uses basically relies on how close the individual buildings are. In the example of a traditional farmstead Figure 2-19, beyond the expressive qualities of the individual building forms, it is apparent that their relationship has been carefully conceived to produce an exterior space capable of supporting specific uses. The realtionship focuses the buildings on a common workyard that has its own microclimate as a result of the enclosure. It is not accidental that the relationship of the buildings creating the space orients toward the south. This provides protection from the prevailing northwesterly winds through the cold winter months, while allowing the southeasterly winds of the summer to keep both the yard and the surrounding buildings cool.

Figure 2-19. Farmstead, Gorham, Maine.

This is an example of a cluster pattern that has created a bowllike containing shape. The space of the farmyard, like the space inside the bowl of the vase, has been produced by the various buildings acting, not as forms, but as defining surfaces. We can describe the bowllike space as a "cluster form." A similar degree of spatial definition within the linear pattern would result if all the breaks were likewise filled in. This would produce a "linear spatial form." These two basic spatial forms can be seen in the plan in Figure 2-20.

Figure 2-18. Elephant house, London Zoo.

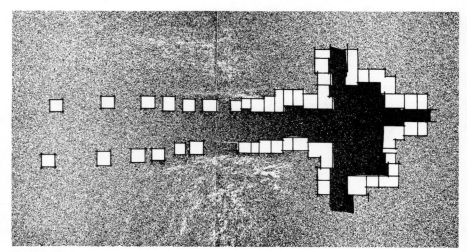
Figure 2-20.

At the start of Part Two, it was suggested that the experience of the urban environment is distinct by virtue of the character and quality of the public domain. In this connection, we suggested that the public domain provides two uniquely urban characteristics: a variety of access modes, and the support of a wide range of other functions and activities.

If we consider the organization of the city at its most elementary level as a question of relationships between people and their activities, in essence relationships concern the location of people and activities in space, time, and distance. The organization of the city might be seen as analogous to the structure of a leaf, with its myriad of cells and an elaborate system of access routes between. It is this system of access that effectively acts as both the life source and the bonding agent that produces the whole (Figure 2-21).

Although the leaf might be an interesting analogy, it fails, however, in describing the urban context in at least two fundamental ways. In the city, the linking system (since it concerns people and not liquids), depends on how well it is supportive of people and their activities. As we have discussed, the most basic of these activities is access. In this respect, the quality of the public domain is in part a function of how well access is accommodated. In this connection, the modern tradition's almost exclusive association of access with the car has had both advantages and disadvantages. The most obvious advantages are greater personal mobility than was possible in traditional pre-modern cities. One of the major disadvantages is that access, other than by car, is limited or impossible, including the most natural and spontaneous (as well as the cheapest); that is, walking. When analyzing the experience of the urban context, the other basic characteristic that specifically distinguishes the traditional city from the open order of the modern tradition is that in the city the public domain not only facilitates a range of access modes, but it is also supportive of many other functions and activities which, in themselves, constitute an important part of the urban experience.

In principle, when, as in the case of the farmyard, buildings are space-defining as well as space-containing elements, the exterior public spaces obtain spatial forms and a quality of their own. The more completely defined the space, the more the spatial form is evident, while the buildings, as defining surfaces, become the background. As with the access and other spaces within buildings, defined spaces outside buildings act as containers for various functions and activities. It is in this sense that the public domain constitutes, in itself, an important part of the urban context.

Figure 2-21.

Beyond the obvious though critical fact that the greater density of cities make a wider range of people, activities, etc., more easily accessible, if experience is a central concern, it becomes evident, as in the case of the farmstead, that the form and disposition of buildings be specifically conceived with the expressive and supportive qualities of the exterior spaces of the public domain and their use in mind. For this purpose it is important to recognize that the character of public spaces relies less on the individual forms of the buildings than on the relationship of buildings as defining surfaces. It is the relationship of surfaces that produced the farmyard and the conditions (including the microclimate) supportive of the various uses to which it is put. The same applies to the city.

the urban environment is distinct by virtue of the character and quality of the public domain

TWO BASIC CATEGORIES OF SPACES WITHIN THE PUBLIC DOMAIN

The importance of access and interaction between human beings, and the extent that the physical environment can play in this, represent some of the most probing questions associated with the city-making task. The attainment of a more sustaining balance between individuals and their social and physical context (natural and built), as discussed earlier, is something people have become increasingly concerned about today.

It must be reemphasized that the basic aim of this book is not that of providing ready-made solutions, but rather to provide tools needed in the decision-making process, insofar as this affects our experience of the city. In this connection, we have seen that there are basically two categories of spaces that can be described as relevant in our experience of the city: linear spaces and cluster spaces.

In his influential book, *Existence, Space and Architecture,* Christian Norberg-Schulz suggested that "taking possession of the environment implies structuring the environment into domains by means of paths and places." Referring to research in structural psychology, and more specifically to the work of the celebrated psychologist Jean Piaget, he argued that these basic forms or "schematas" are fundamental to the way we adapt and modify the physical environment to human purpose. This is also consistent with the earlier work of Kevin Lynch, in which he sought to identify the physical characteristics that make the urban context understandable and meaningful to people. In his research he found that paths and nodes, among other characteristics, are critical to people's image of the city. Orientation within and use of the city seem to be strongly associated with and reliant upon the "imageability" that is in part based on these characteristics.[5]

In the dual role of accommodating access and supporting other functions and activities, we can generalize by saying that historiccally, the public domain of the city has consisted of the two basic categories of linear and cluster spatial forms. These two forms are, for example, what basically comprise the public domain in the plan in Figure 2-22.

In the following pages, we will examine more closely how these two basic categories of spatial forms operate as sources of information, providing both expressive and supportive qualities in the public domain of the city.

Figure 2-22. Strasbourg, France

Linear Spaces

The first category of spatial forms upon which our understanding and use of the city relies corresponds to the access corridors within buildings. Like these, linear spaces in the city are expressive and supportive of the most basic aspect of the urban experience that concerns linkage and access. As Norberg-Schulz suggested, "how we get from one place to another is a basic aspect of man's being in the world."

As within buildings, the character and quality of linear access spaces are critical to the role they play and the nature of our experience. In this connection, under Component One, we will consider three basic variables that affect the character and quality of linear spaces: shape, scale, and the organization of the defining surfaces. The "use value" of the city street, unlike building corridors, concerns the range of access modes it permits and facilitates. This, in part, relies on these variables. The coordination of and relationship of activities within buildings that define linear spaces, as well as the treatment of the spaces themselves, Components Two and Three, together determine the full range of uses that can occur there. At this point our discussion will be limited to the analysis of how linear spaces as spatial forms provide us with basic use-oriented information.

Figure 2-23. Logan Airport, Boston, Massachusetts.

Figure 2-24. Ship Street, Oxford, England.

like corridors inside buildings

The Effects of Perspective in Our Experience of the City. Before examining in more detail how the linear spatial forms produced by the surfaces of buildings provide both expressive and supportive conditions in the public domain, we will briefly consider how perspective functions in our experience of the physical environment in general.

In principle, we never see the world as it actually is. Rather we see it from one position and relative to ourselves. The basic laws of perspective merely summarize the fact that our relationship to the world around us is fundamentally reliant on our understanding of distance. Distance is expressed by the fact that as things get farther from us, they get visually smaller, though constant in actual size. As the French philosopher Maurice Merleau-Ponty explained in his seminal book, *Phenomenology of Perception,* "It is the apparent size of (objects) which, relative to their real size, assigns to them their place in space."[6]

In the example of a simple country road in Figure 2-25 because we relate to our environment "in terms of the way we use it," we tend to interpret and "translate" the shrinking caused by perspective in practical terms. The shrinking suggests distance and implies that a certain quantity of time will be required to traverse it. It is in this sense that "distance is time made rigid."

Thus, although the road is fixed and immobile, we tend to read it in action terms. Just as the eye "moves" and "extends," reaching out toward the horizon along the paved surface, so too the road is seen as moving and extending out toward the horizon. In this connection, one could say that seeing is the most elementary form of extension beyond the grasping hand.

Both the movement of the eye as well as the basic action quality of the road can be represented in diagrammatic form using a simple vector sketch, as in Figure 2-26. The vector can be described as an interpretation of the road's dynamic expressive quality as it relates to use.

Figure 2-25. Prince Edward Island, Canada.

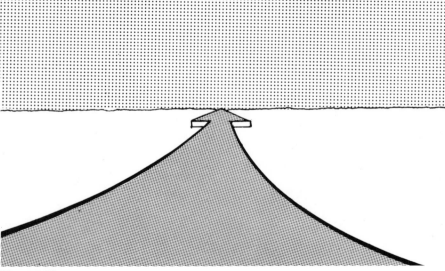

Figure 2-26.

form is "translated" in action terms

Perspective and Buildings. If we turn to a linear pattern of buildings, we find that the effect of visual distortion, associated with perspective, has similar "action" implications. In general, we never see a building straight on. Rather we see buildings from an angle, and as such their form is distorted by perspective (see Figure 2-27). In principle, perspective distorts buildings in the same way that it distorted our country road, i.e., they get smaller and shrink as they "move" away from us.

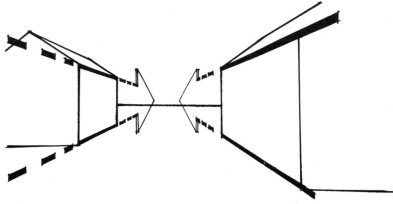

Figure 2-27.

Within a linear pattern of buildings, as in Figure 2-28, the distortion of perspective carries on from one building to the next. The gradual shrinking of the surfaces actually tends to link the buildings together, and a directional quality is produced (Figure 2-29). This quality is meaningful to us, not only because it is expressive of distance, but because, as with our country road, it is expressive of a functional purpose.

The significance of this linear relationship of building forms provides information that goes beyond the meaning of the individual buildings. The relationship of the forms, as it effects both visual and actual experience, is indicative of a larger order. It is indicative in that it expresses an intention with regards to how the public domain is meant to be used. More specifically, it expresses how these individual buildings are linked and how we can gain access from one to another.

Figure 2-28. Williamsburg, Virginia.

Figure 2-29.

perspective is associated with distance and time

Spatial Forms and "Use Messages." Moving now to the case of linear spaces, as in the pedestrian passage in central Oxford (Figure 2-30), we can see how the relationship of the surfaces effects perception and interpretation. As in the case of linear patterns, the linear organization and relationship of the defining surfaces are perceived through the distortions of perspective. The shrinking of the surfaces is associated in our minds with distance and it is upon this that our interpretation is based. The total enclosure and clarity of the surface relationships (Figure 2-31a) provides us with a distinct spatial figure or form (Figure 2-31b). As in a corridor, it is this that we basically respond to as much as the surfaces that create it.

The interpretive process, as we have suggested, is in essence a process of "translation." Not only do we perceive the space itself as moving, but we tend to translate the form into "use messages," which it provides. Described in simple terms, the basic linear shape of this space, like the neck of our vase, places it clearly in our first category of spatial types. It is unquestionably meant for movement and there is no ambiguity about it. If it came to a dead end as we walked down, thus negating its apparent access function, we would be both surprised and frustrated.

If our interpretation of space is directly related to use, then the overall "use messages," beyond shape, concern the overall scale relative to the size of our

Figure 2-30. Bulwarks Lane, Oxford, England.

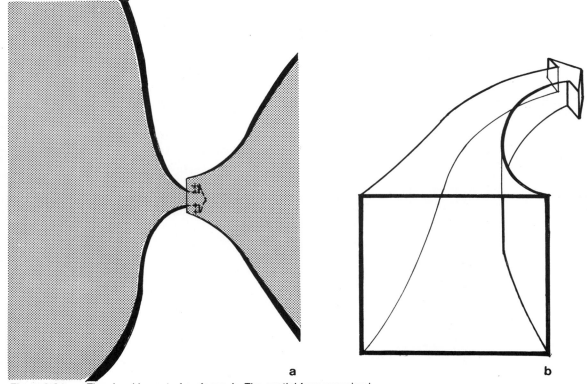

a

b

Figure 2-31. a. The visual impact of surfaces. b. The spatial form perceived.

bodies and our ability to move. This is the *only* basis that provides us with an objective standard for assessing our environment. It is for this reason that, as in the example of a miniature village in England in Figure 2-32, people have little difficulty in understanding scale models. These have been and remain perhaps the most effective devices for simulating and communicating development proposals.

In this connection, as in the sketch in Figure 2-33, it is the overall scale, as determined by height, width, and length relative to people, that provides the use messages. In addition to the ratio of height to width, the scale in absolute terms suggests modes of use. This is associated with both visual interest and the time required to move the length. Thus, in general, the larger the space relative to the human scale, the more rapidly we are inclined to move. Spaces that are much larger than required by the human scale suggest mechanical means of movement.

Limiting our discussion at this point to the question of height and width and the ratio between them, we can see that these two variables alone greatly affect the character of linear spaces. Variations in the ratio of height to width strongly determine the sense of enclosure that one experiences.

Figure 2-33. The human reference as basis for scale.

Figure 2-32. Model village, Portsmouth, England.

the human scale provides the basic reference

In the various sections in Figure 2-35, we might characterize and associate different ratios with different feelings produced. Where the ratio exceeds 2 to 1, as in the examples in Barcelona and New York (Figures 2-34 and 2-36), a sense of claustrophobia is often experienced. This, in part, results from the fact that the vertical perspective produces an illusion of buildings closing in overhead.

The feelings associated with the ratio of height to width are not universal and will vary from one cultural setting and era to another. More important, however, as discussed in the preceding page, is the actual scale of spaces relative to human beings.

Many of the earlier attempts at developing planning legislation, going back to Ancient Rome, were aimed at controlling the oppressive effects of high-density development.

Figure 2-36. New York City's financial district.

Figure 2-34. The Gothic Quarter, Barcelona, Spain.

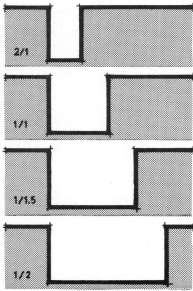

2/1

1/1

1/1.5

1/2

Figure 2-35. Height to width ratios.

the height to width ratio greatly affects the character of linear spaces

Various techniqes for controlling the effect of tall buildings on the public domain have been used. These include the use of height setbacks so as to maintain the street scale and to permit more sunlight to reach ground level.

The Empire State Building in New York City (Figure 2-39) is an example of this type of control. While the tower rises to a height of 102 stories, the character of Fifth Avenue as a space has been maintained. More recently, similar development controls have been applied in other parts of the city. In examples on Second Avenue and Broadway (Figures 2-37 and 2-38), street definition and scale has been maintained through required building lines and height setbacks in the street facades. In the Broadway example an arcade was also required at the street level.

Such development controls in New York and other places are rapidly being recognized as essential in the development of more coherent building form insofar as this affects the public domain.[7]

Figure 2-39. Empire State Building, New York City.

Figure 2-37. Second Avenue, New York City.

Figure 2-38. Broadway, New York City.

the control of high density to maintain the street

Changes in the scale of spaces perceived, beyond height and width, also relies on length. The use of curvilinear patterns in street plans, as in the example of Edinburgh (Figure 2-41), can be very effective. Other useful devices include bends and building projections, as in cases in Athens and Paris in Figures 2-40 and 2-42. In his classic work, *Townscape,* Gordon Cullen has referred to such design/planning techniques with regards to the length of space perceived as ways of producing "closure." The example of a local street in Brighton, England (Figures 2-43 and 2-44), achieves much of its delight as a result of the closure produced by a curvilinear layout that provides a highly human scale.[8]

A more dramatic and equally effective technique for the modification of the scale of linear spaces is that of bridging over streets with linking structures or entire buildings. Older use of this "air rights" technique, include an example in the city of Rhodes on the Greek island and a pedestrian link of Venetian influence in Oxford (Figures 2-45 and 2-46). A contemporary example of air rights is the Fashion Institute of Technology in New York (Figure 2-47).

Figure 2-40. Athens, Greece (the Plaka district).

Figure 2-41. Edinburgh, Scotland (Moray Place).

Figure 2-42. Paris, France (Le Marais district).

Figure 2-43. Brighton, England (The Lanes district).

Figure 2-44.

Figure 2-45. New College Lane, Oxford, England.

Figure 2-46. Rhodes, Greece.

Figure 2-47. Fashion Institute of Technology, New York City.

The Organization of Defining Surfaces. In the preceding section, we considered how the character of linear spaces is heavily reliant on their shape and scale as perceived at any point along the way. Variations in the width and length of spaces, as well as in the height of the defining surfaces, provides the basic vocabulary of the visual language of linear spaces.

In this section of our analysis, we consider how the architectural organization of the individual facades also affects the scale of linear spaces. In principle we have seen that the scale of linear spaces and the suggested modes of use are interrelated. Beyond this, the scale of linear spaces is also affected by the quantity of visual stimulis, or information, provided within the defining surfaces. In general, within building surfaces, features that counter the sense of horizontal movement are "translated" within the total use message of the space defined as suggesting that physical movement be slower. The more horizontal surfaces are vertically broken the less rapidly the spanning movement of the eye will "extend" down the space. As Gordon Cullen has suggested, because of this, interest remains close to the viewer, and the "here" is as important as the "there."[9]

Clearly the most important source for this additional visual information is provided by the openings in the defining surfaces: windows and doors; that is, Component Two. With regard to the basic definition of space, however, visual breaks can also be achieved within the organization of building surfaces.

In the example in Figure 2-48 (once a service street in Oxford), minor variations in the alignment and height of buildings modify the simple linearity of the space. In the analytic sketch in Figure 2-49, we can see that, although the basic relationship of the building surfaces still produces a clear and "legible" linear spatial form, the variations mentioned above serve to counteract and modify the sense of movement. The basic access function of the space remains apparent, but the character is passive and low-key. The "journey" of the eye, as it is ultimately translated in terms of our actual movement through the space is represented by the meandering ground vector shown.

In terms of use, the intimate and supportive character of this space is well suited to the kind of local commercial role it has spontaneously developed in recent years.

Figure 2-48. Parade Avenue, Oxford, England.

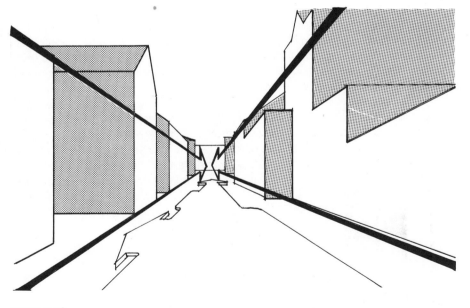

Figure 2-49.

81

Horizontal/Vertical Organization. Variations in alignment and height in the organization of facades can be described very simply in terms of vertical and horizontal emphasis. In general, we can say that horizontal organization tends to be directional and movement oriented, while vertical organization, which draws the eye up and in opposition to horizontal movement, is more static.

In two contrasting examples (Figure 2-50 and 2-51), the vertical/horizontal organization of the building surfaces has a large impact on the character of the spaces they define. In the case of residential buildings along Commonwealth Avenue in Boston (Figure 2-50), there is a strong vertical emphasis in the organization of the facades. In contrast, the example of a building on Massachusetts Avenue, also in Boston (Figure 2-51), has a strong horizontal emphasis in its organization.

As can be seen in the following analytic sketches the difference in emphasis in the vertical/horizontal organization of the surfaces has a clear impact on the character of the spaces defined. In the example of a street in Canterbury, England (Figures 2-52 and 2-53), a strong horizontal organization was used in the new building on the left. The older buildings on the right, in contrast, have a strong vertical organization. The effects that such differences in organization can have in spaces is more evident in two other cases also in England. The first is a pedestrian mall in the town of Stevenage (Figure 2-54 and 2-55). Here the horizontal movement in the facades is very strong. In the second case, London Street in Norwich, the organization has a strong vertical emphasis (Figure 2-56 and 2-57). Although the spaces in these two contrasting examples are very similar in their basic shape and scale, the movement of the eye and the suggested modes of usage are very different. Whereas the movement of the eye in Stevenage receives little opposition in the defining surfaces, strong opposition occurs in the Norwich case. In terms of the effect this has in our use of these spaces, the first suggests and invites a rapidity of movement that one could say is inconsistent with the actual pedestrian treatment and use intended. In contrast, the second case, which is a street that was pedestrianized, the visual complexity provided by the vertical breaks contributes to a more passive quality consistent with the pedestrian mode of use intended. The form and content are complementary and their combination is highly supportive.

the vertical/horizontal organization of surfaces

Figure 2-50. Commonwealth Avenue, Boston, Massachusetts.

Figure 2-51. Massachusetts Avenue, Boston, Massachusetts.

Figure 2-52. Mercery Lane, Canterbury, England.

Figure 2-53.

Figure 2-54. Market Walk, Stevenage new town, England.

Figure 2-55.

Figure 2-56. London Street, Norwich, England.

Figure 2-57.

Respect for the scale and organization of existing streets, as design and development factors, has again become evident in a number of new buildings in recent years. Examples of distinctly twentieth-century buildings, where the basic scale and character of a street has been maintained, represent an important trend away from the kind of isolated buildings associated with the modern tradition.

In the example of new residential buildings in an old sector of Strasbourg, France (Figure 2-59), an emphasis on vertical organization has been provided in order to maintain the scale and visual character of the medieval street. A residential development in Oxford (Figure 2-60) has similar qualities. Another example of this type of response to the character of existing streets is a new building for the National Guard in New York (Figure 2-58). Here again, the formal street definition has been maintained as well as the scale and rhythm of existing adjacent buildings. This shows how the richness of the small parcel development of earlier eras need not be lost in the development of larger parcels, as is more typical today.

Figure 2-59. Strasbourg, France (Petite France district).

Figure 2-58. National Guard Armory, New York City.

Figure 2-60. Housing, Oxford, England.

Other Defining Elements. Of great importance in our analysis of urban spaces is the role surfaces other than buildings can have in defining space. The use of walls, fences, etc., for the enclosure of private and utilitarian spaces, as in Figures 2-61 to 2-63, can be very effective.

Of equal and perhaps greater importance in the definition of space is the use of greenery. Because of the density that can be achieved with hedges, trees, etc., their value as basic design elements in achieving definition for the public domain cannot be overestimated. The most important among these is the use of trees. While providing a sense of balance between the man-made and natural environment, trees can and have historically contributed to the production of meaningful public spaces.

The examples in Figures 2-64 to 2-66 demonstrate various situations where shrubs, trees, etc., provide a distinct sense of spatial definition.

Figure 2-61. Greenwich Village, New York City.

Figure 2-62. Paris (Le Marais district).

Figure 2-63. Stoe on the Wold, Oxfordshire, England.

the use of other defining surfaces

87

Figure 2-64. Oxford, England.

Figure 2-66. Athens, Greece.

Figure 2-65. New York City.

The Expressive Quality of Towers. In our discussion of built forms at the start of this section, towers were described as expressions of an upward "reach" in the defiance of gravity. As such, they have historically functioned as symbols of faith, power, etc. Within the urban context, they are also indications of centrality, land values, etc. Thus, as forms, towers have historically acted as both signs and symbols in our experience of the city.

Cathedral towers, as in Norwich, England (Figure 2-67) are beacons that act as symbolic expressions of a hierarchy of values, while being indicative of centrality in the structure of the city. They mark the center of the city and symbolize the highest value shared by the community. In practical terms, the height of the tower, as with minarets in Islamic countries, made it possible for the sound of bells (or chanting) to reach the faithful within and beyond the city, thus, an early form of long-distance communication.

In modern times, as in the center of New York City (Figure 2-68), towers still retain the expressive qualities of power, centrality, etc. When judiciously used in conjunction with a center, as in the new town of Reston in Virginia (Figures 2-69, 2-70), towers can still retain an important functional and symbolic role in providing a sense of orientation and hierarchy in the overall form of a development.

Figure 2-68. Manhattan from Brooklyn, New York City.

Figure 2-67. Norwich, England.

towers act as both signs and symbols

Figure 2-69. Lake Ann Center Square.

Figure 2-70. Reston, Virginia, Lake Ann Center.

Within the context of linear spaces, towers have a strong modifying affect on both the journey of the eye and the character of spaces percieved. In principle, as with the vertical organization of surfaces discussed earlier, vertical masses temporarily stop the horizontal progression of the eye and turn it upwards. The high visibility of a tower thus punctuates the space, and in so doing, has the effect of subdividing it into distinct sections. Not only does this increase the visual complexity and interest of the space, but symbolically it greatly increases its importance.

This is particularly evident in the examples on this and the following pages. In central city streets in Glasgow, Scotland (Figure 2-71), and in Steyr, Austria (Figure 2-72), towers modulate the spaces while providing focal elements that symbolically emphasize the importance of these streets.

Figure 2-71. Argyle Street, Glasgow, Scotland.

Figure 2-72. Sierninger strasse, Steyr, Austria.

towers punctuate and give symbolic importance to streets

91

As indicated in the analytic sketches overlaying the photos in Figures 2-74 and 2-76, although the basic organization of the defining surfaces seen in perspective (heavy line) produces and maintains distinct, unambiguous and clearly "legible" linear spaces, in each case the use of one or more towers carries the movement of the eye (thin dashed line) upward and in opposition to the dominant horizontal movement of the street space.

In the example of the ancient Berber town of Ouarzazat (Figure 2-73), the horizontal massing of the residential buildings (and the blankness of the walls) is contrasted by the dominance of a taller building. Historically the residence of the town's feudal lord, this building not only acted as a symbol of power, but also provided the labyrinthine system of streets with an essential orientation element. The same organizational qualities were achieved in medieval closed-order towns, while in the later Renaissance period (structured order) this became an important characteristic of city-building.

In the case of High Street in Oxford in Figures 2-75, 2-76, a series of towers, associated with the different university colleges, provides a strong processional rhythm, while emphasizing the importance of the street as the most important public space in the city.

Figure 2-74.

Figure 2-73. Ouarzazat, Morocco.

the horizontal movement is counteracted while increasing the orientational quality of the street

92

Figure 2-75. High Street, Oxford, England.

Figure 2-76.

Hierarchy in Linear Spaces. With the variables of shape, scale and density of visual information discussed in the preceding section, a wide range of linear spaces can be produced. As we have seen the basic use that linear spaces suggest (through their use messages) is a function of these variables. Thus, different modes of use, in terms of access, are suggested. This ranges from very rapid vehicular movement to very passive and local pedestrian movement.

The differences that linear spaces have in terms of the variables discussed affect our understanding and use, not only of individual linear spaces, but also our understanding and use of cities in general. Different scales of linear spaces are associated both functionally and symbolically with the city at different "levels." This ranges from the city level to the most intimate, the block level. As parts of a total access system, various scales of linear spaces provide the city with a hierarchy that makes the organization of a city plan understandable.

In this connection, utilizing the simple plan in Figure 2-77, we can discern three basic levels of linear spaces. Level A concerns linear spaces at the city level; Level B concerns linear spaces at the sector level (or neighborhood); Level C concerns linear spaces at the block level.

City Level. Linear spaces at the city level provide the basic system upon which access through or across the whole of the city relies. It is also upon this system that we depend for our basic conception of and orientation within the city. The boulevards of Paris (Figure 2-78), built under the direction of Baron Haussman in the mid-nineteenth century, provide the previously medieval city structure with a system of access at the city level.

The structured order of the Renaissance and Baroque periods depended largely on these city-level linear spaces for the organization of cities as both functionally and visually unified structures. Within the gridiron plan of New York, the city-level system is provided by the major north-south avenues (Figure 2-79). Like the boulevards of Paris, their spatial character and scale clearly distinguishes them from the secondary and more local east-west streets. In both Paris and New York, it is consistent to find that higher densities and the more important civic functions (libraries, major stores, opera houses, etc.), as well as public transport systems, are directly associated with these city-level streets.

Figure 2-77.

Figure 2-78. Boulevard Henri IV, Paris, France.

When additional elements like arcades, trees, street furniture, etc., are introduced within these city-level spaces, as will be discussed under Components Two and Three, they become supportive of a wide range of functions and activities in addition to through-city access.

Though acting as boundaries for the various sectors of the city, these spaces, as in the example in Paris (Figure 2-81), also function as major focuses of activity and "interface" between sectors.

The importance of city-level linear spaces, as multifunction components of the city structure, has been largely underrated and often lost in modern city-planning. Total segregation of access modes, as in the use of modern highways, is undoubtedly relevant outside and between cities as well as at points of extreme density and congestion. Within the urban context, however, they often have a fragmenting and segregating effect that contradicts the multifunctional nature of the city.

Figure 2-79. Madison Avenue, New York City.

Figure 2-80. Typical city-level

street section (H/W ratio of 1/2).

Figure 2-81. Rue St. Antoine, Paris, France.

city-level streets provide the basic access and orientation system in the city

City-level linear spaces, as major organizational elements, need not always or necessarily be major traffic arteries like the boulevards of Paris or the avenues of New York. City-level linear spaces can also be major amenity spaces.

Excellent examples of this include the Ramblas in Barcelona (Figure 1-56), where the central portion of the space (where the city wall once stood) is a promenade. Here one finds cafes and a variety of kiosks selling flowers, newspapers, etc., both day and night.

Commonwealth Avenue in Boston (Figures 2-82 and 2-50), is an example of how a major linear space at the city level can be an important structuring component and also a major amenity. Another example of this kind of dual role is the boulevard Jules Ferry (Figures 2-83, 1-73, and 1-84), where a deck, built over portions of a canal, provides a variety of recreational facilities for the surrounding neighborhoods.

In general, any city-level linear space that is heavily planted, as in the example in Fes, Morocco (Figure 2-84) also acts as a linear park while giving a strong sense of cohesion to the city. Many of the boulevards of Paris were originally lined with two or three rows of trees on each side, thus providing this amenity quality.

Figure 2-83. Boulevard Jules Ferry, Paris, France.

Figure 2-82. Commonwealth Avenue, Boston, Massachusetts.

Figure 2-84. Fez, Morocco.

Sector Level.   Our second level of linear spaces includes a very wide range of streets. In principle, however, their main function is associated with access at the scale of the sector or neighborhood. Smaller and more intimate in scale, this class of linear spaces is well suited to the more local and passive access activities that naturally occur at this level of the city. Vehicular movement in these spaces, in contrast to city level spaces, is ideally moderated to coexist and share the space rather than dominate it.

The intimate quality of most medieval cities, as in Lewis, England (Figure 2-85), or Rouen, France (Figure 2-86) is largely dependant on this scale of linear space. The cases in Figures 2-40 to 2-49 are also examples of sector-level linear spaces. In Figures 2-87 to 2-89 are three highly successful sector-level spaces in New York, Philadelphia, and St. Malo. In each case, a strong sense of identity with the street as an extension of one's personal space is generally experienced.

Figure 2-85. Lewis, England.

Figure 2-86. Rouen, France.

sector-level streets are more suited to the local activities of the neighborhood

Figure 2-87. Philadelphia, Pennsylvania.

Figure 2-89. St. Malo, France.

Figure 2-88. Greenwich Village, New York City.

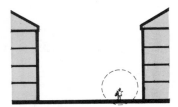

Figure 2-90. Typical sector-level
street section (H/W ratio of 1/1.5).

a strong sense of identity is experienced

Block—Level. The third class of linear spaces functions at the most intimate urban level. Its main function is to provide access through and within the individual city blocks. In general, it serves for pedestrian use.

The case in Oxford (Figure 2-30), and in the village of Stowe (Figure 2-63), are examples of such spaces serving for local pedestrian access. In ancient and early medieval cities, however, this highly intimate class of linear space frequently comprised much of the street system of cities. The cases of Ouarzazat (Figure 2-73) and the medieval city of Rhodes (Figure 2-46) are both examples of this, as are the cities of Mykonos, Fes, and Venice (Figures 2-91 to 2-94).

Contemporary examples of such linear spaces, in New Haven and Philadelphia (Figures 2-95 to 2-98), are highly effective in providing the intimate "fine grain" upon which the supportive quality of the city relies.

Figure 2-94. Venice.

Figure 2-91. Mykonos, Greece.

Figure 2-92. Fez, Morocco.

Figure 2-93. Mykonos, Greece.

block-level streets are well suited for pedestrian-only use

Figure 2-95. Philadelphia, Pennsylvania.

Figure 2-96,97. New Haven, Connecticut.

Figure 2-98. Access lane, Philadelphia, Pennsylvania.

Figure 2-99. Typical block-level street section (H/W ratio of 1/1).

highly effective in providing the "fine grain" access within city blocks

Block Level, Commercial.   Within the block-level class of linear spaces, particular mention should be made of their use within central-city situations. In terms of the supportive quality of their scale, block-level linear spaces lend themselves easily to commercial roles. This explains why many of the older city centers of Europe, like in London (Figure 2-102), have been so easily and successfully transformed into pedestrian districts. Besides a bollard here and there, few additional modifications are needed to make the new role "a natural."

The value of block-level linear spaces in reducing the scale of large central-city plans down to human (and walkable) scale, cannot be overestimated as in a 19th-century example of a "mid-block" connection in central London (Figure 2-100). With the help of a few trees and benches, as in a new development in Williamsburg, Virginia (Figure 2-101), modern central cities can provide highly supportive qualities as well as the intimate scale of older cities.

Figure 2-102. Commercial alley, London's West End district.

Figure 2-100. Sicilian Avenue, London, England

Figure 2-101. Williamsburg, Virginia.

block-level streets lend themselves naturally to central-city commerical roles

101

The current fashion of pedestrianizing major "city-level" streets in the center of cities can often be problematic because of basic spatial contradictions. In terms of spatial use messages, large spaces do not suggest passive pedestrian-only activities. Major spatial modifications, with the use of trees, street furniture, etc., as in central Munich (Figure 2-103), or very large numbers of people, as in a temporary closure of New York's Fifth Avenue, (Figure 2-104), are essential in making such large spaces work.

Where cultural and climatic conditions are favorable and the necessary support systems of access, parking and zoning controls are provided (eliminating competition from outlying shopping centers), large pedestrian spaces have been successful. In addition to the spatial contradictions mentioned above, however, the removal of major city-level routes has often led to a debatable restriction on the multiple role of major central-city streets. The use of the city relies on spaces both as places and as part of a system. Eliminating access on a "city-level" street is a major decision having many repercussions throughout the system.

Figure 2-104. Fifth Avenue, New York City.

Figure 2-103. Neuhauser Strasse, Munich, Germany.

city-level streets can but do not easily lend themselves to pedestrian-only use

Cluster Spaces

The second basic category of spatial forms upon which our experience of the urban context relies, the "cluster space," like the bowl of our vase and rooms inside buildings, are expressive of containment.

Similar to linear spaces, cluster spaces are concerned with access and linkage, but unlike linear spaces, access and linkage do not constitute the principal function of these spaces. As "clusters" of both buildings and activities, the basic function of cluster spaces is that of providing supports for the "overlap and interaction" of people and activities. Like the buildings that act as individual containers, cluster spaces also function as containers. In contrast, however, these are totally public and offer the greatest opportunity for people to come together as a community. While the basic containing space of the room can be described as the most elementary extension of the human body and, to quote Christian Norberg-Schulz, "man's first real attempt to take possession of the environment," the exterior cluster space can be described in similar terms but for the social body rather than the individual.

In his discussion of public spaces, Mr. Norberg-Schulz suggested that the tradition of clustering buildings, creating the distinct gathering spaces found throughout history, "indicate that natural space is never enough to concretize man's existential space. Even the nomads group their tents." Paul Zucker, in his book, *Town and Square,* explained that sociologically, "only within a civilization where the anonymous human being had become a 'citizen,' where democracy had unfolded to some extent, could the gathering place become important enough to take on a specific shape."

The role cluster spaces have within the urban context depends on several factors. As with linear spaces, these include shape, scale, and visual information. To a large extent these determine the importance of focal spaces in the urban hierarchy. Of equal importance, however, is the way focal spaces relate to the structure of linear spaces. As with rooms inside buildings, the location of cluster spaces within the city and their relationship to the access system, strongly determines their use.

Figure 2-105.

cluster spaces act as containers for the overlap and interaction of people and activities

Building Relationships, Perspective and Use Messages. The relationship of buildings as defining surfaces, when seen in perspective, largely determine the uses that cluster spaces suggest. As with linear spaces, the spatial forms of cluster spaces are perceived in dynamic and practical terms.

In principle, our "reading" of a cluster space relies on the basic fact that the relationship of the defining surfaces produces "enclosure." The movement of the eye, unlike with linear spaces, is not directed away from the viewer, but "around." The principle effect of the surface relationships is that of concentrating attention on a distinct and static roomlike spatial form. Like a room inside a building, the existence of cluster spaces absolutely relies on the defining surfaces, and when these are lacking or incomplete, the form loses its definition. The cluster does not "take place."

In the example in Figure 2-106, the effects of the relationships between the defining surfaces of cluster spaces can be seen. Here a simple linear space, a street of the industrial era in England, has been transformed by local inhab-

itants into a makeshift cluster space for the purposes of providing a gathering place (the occasion of the Queen's jubilee in 1977). The transformation has been achieved by the simple stretching of a canvas across the street. Analytically, the effect of this, as indicated in Figure 2-107, is to counter the directional movement of the street while the eye instead moves around and circles the viewer. This example demonstrates the way the expressive qualities of cluster spaces are associated with particular types of uses.

The small opening that has been left in one corner of the space provides an essential link between the surrounding community and the space. In terms of the defining surfaces, this break can be described as a visual "leak" in the sense that the eye is allowed to "move out" of the space. This does not, however, compromise the basic spatial form of the space.

When the number of breaks in the defining surfaces becomes excessive, as mentioned above, the sense of spatial definition and containment is lost. The effect of breaks will be further examined in the following pages.

Figure 2-106. Portsmouth, England.

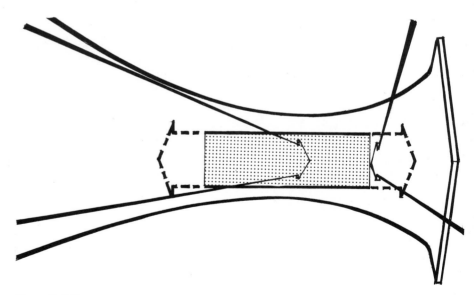

Figure 2-107.

As with linear spaces, the form of cluster spaces, determined by shape, scale, and organization of defining surfaces, determines the basic use messages produced. In principle, simple shapes, like squares, rectangles, and circles, permit rapid visual exploration from any position within a space. As such, they are more formal and have historically been used where a clear symbolic expression of place was sought. In contrast, oblong and more complicated shapes invite and indeed require visual exploration, which generally involves physical displacement of the viewer. Such spaces are generally more informal in character and can lend themselves more naturally to a variety of uses than do squares with simple shapes.

Relative to the human body, the scale of cluster spaces strongly influences the kinds of uses suggested. Whereas smaller spaces, as in the example of a local plaza within a residential development in New York (Figure 2-109 and 2-108a), are intimate and well suited to a local role, larger spaces, as in the example of a major square in Salzburg in Figure 2-110 and 2-108b are more naturally suited for major city-level roles. This will of course be influenced by the uses housed within the containing buildings, as well as the location and relationship of the space within the context of the urban structure and the specific treatment of the space (Component Three).

Figure 2-109. Southbridge Towers Plaza, New York City.

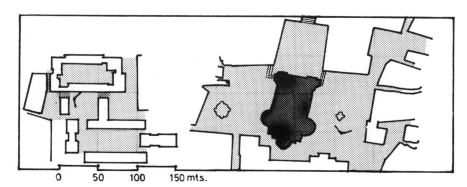

0   50   100   150 mts.

Figure 2-108. a. Southbridge Towers, New York. b. Central squares, Salzburg, Austria.

the scale of cluster spaces strongly influences the kinds of uses suggested

Figure 2-110. Residenzplatz, Salzburg, Austria.

105

Other Defining Surfaces. The definition of cluster spaces need not, anymore than linear spaces, rely exclusively on buildings. Other surfaces, like walls, fences, hedges, colonnades and trees, can all provide varying degrees of definition. In conjunction with buildings, these various devices can provide the kind of distinct spatial form discussed earlier.

In the example of the large twelve-acre square in front of the new city hall in Toronto (Nathan Phillips' Square, Figure 2-111,a,b), the use of a raised walkway helps to delineate and provide a sense of enclosure not otherwise provided by buildings. In the examples of St. Peter's Square in Rome, and the courtyards behind the Palais Royal in Paris (Figures 2-112,113), the definition of these cluster spaces relies very heavily on the use of colonnades.

Figure 2-112. St. Peter's Square, arcade, Rome.

Figure 2-111, a.b. Nathan Phillips' Square, Toronto, Canada.

Figure 2-113. Garden courtyards, Palais Royal, Paris.

the definition of cluster spaces need not rely exclusively on buildings

The Organization of Defining Surfaces and the Effects of Towers. As with linear spaces, the scale and character of cluster spaces is affected by the basic organization of defining surfaces. Thus, the emphasis on vertical and horizontal elements influences the journey of the eye around the space. In principle, an emphasis on vertical organization, as in the example in Steyr, Austria (Figure 2-114), retards the sweeping movement of the eye and provides a great deal of visual complexity. This modifies the scale and character of the space, making it more informal and visually "busy." The visual effect is summarized in the analytic sketch in Figure 2-115.

The visual and symbolic effects of towers in cluster spaces generally are considerable. As discussed earlier, the freestanding quality of towers tends to arrest the horizontal outreach and exploration of the eye, while drawing attention to one stationary and nondirectional location. Towers have the double effect of drawing our attention out and away from the space itself while simultaneously emphasizing the importance and the role of the space as a focus in the city. As such, towers can complement cluster spaces in their expressive and supportive qualities.

The importance of towers, as expressions and symbols of urban focus within cluster spaces, has been a recognized feature of cities throughout history. The use of towers is particularly effective and meaningful in our experience when they are associated with important civic functions as in cathedrals, town halls, etc. In such cases, this provides a high level of consistency between form and content. The example in Figure 2-116 in Arras, France, is a classic demonstration of this use. The accompanying analytic sketch (Figure 2-117) shows how the tower produces the visual impact that produces the symbolic qualities associated with the use of towers in cluster spaces.

Figure 2-114. Stadtplatz, Steyr, Austria.

Figure 2-115.

107

Figure 2-116. Petite Place, Arras, France.

Figure 2-117.

108

Linkage and Hierarchy; Three Basic Classes of Cluster Spaces.
Cluster spaces operate on different urban levels which, as with linear spaces, are related to scale. The larger spaces are supportive of major city-level functions, while the smaller and more intimate spaces are better suited for sector and local needs.

In contrast to linear spaces, which traverse and "move" across the city, cluster spaces rely heavily on their location and relationship within the city structure and system of linear spaces. Their importance within the hierarchy of the city, in addition to shape and scale, thus depends on the way they are linked with the surrounding city.

In a modified version of the city plan used in our earlier discussion of linear spaces (Figure 2-118), we will consider three basic classes of cluster spaces: the first class (A), like a room, is totally enclosed and only indirectly linked with the surrounding city. This class will be referred to as "inverted spaces." The second class (B), in strong contrast to the first, is clearly linked into the city's system of linear spaces. Often located at an important overlap or "crossroads" of linear spaces, as in our plan, these spaces will be referred to as strategic spaces.

In the third class of cluster spaces (C), characteristics of the first two classes are combined. Providing a strong sense of enclosure, they are also well linked to the system of linear spaces. We will refer to these as "compound spaces."

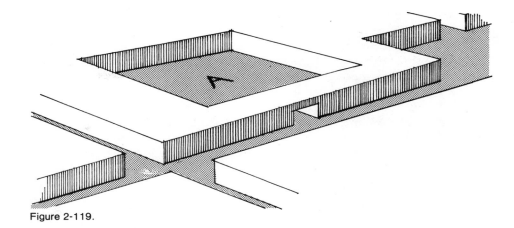

Figure 2-119.

Inverted Spaces. The first class of cluster spaces most closely approximates the interior rooms of buildings. Like the space in our plan (and Figure 2-119), they are enclosed without any major breaks in the defining surfaces. Entered like rooms through portals, the relationship of such spaces to the city is only indirect. As such, the activities and movements in the surrounding streets do not "flow" into or strongly influence the use of these spaces.

The importance and role of inverted spaces within the structure and hierarchy of the public domain of the city depends strongly on their scale and location within the city. Because their access function is limited, the uses housed within its defining buildings, as well as the activities brought within the space itself, are also critical in determining the role they have in the city.

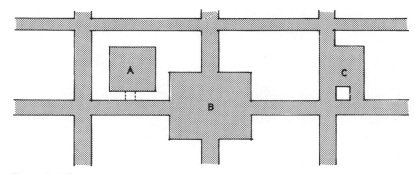

Figure 2-118.

Early examples of inverted spaces were the Imperial forums of classical Rome (Figure 2-120, upper center). Conceived and built by successive emperors, each was in fact a formal outdoor room, isolated and cut off from the busy street life of the city beyond. Their role was highly symbolic and their use was largely limited to planned activities and formal events.

Later derivatives of Roman forums were the contemplative cloister spaces and ''quads'' of European monasteries and early colleges. The central space at King's College, Cambridge University, is an example of this (Figure 2-121).

On a grander scale and more central in the public life of cities were the later and numerous royal squares build throughout Europe from the seventeenth century on. The enormous Place des Vosges in Paris, built in 1615 (Figure 2-122), as well as the Plaza Real in Barcelona (Figure 2-123) are examples of such inverted cluster spaces. A unique example of this class of cluster spaces in the United States is the central space at the University of Virginia in Charlottesville (Figure 2-124). With a direct lineage back to Roman forums, this space is surrounded by a colonnade through which most of the circulation is channeled.

Links between these spaces and the surrounding city, as in the example of an entrance to Place des Vosges (Figure 2-125), are generally small and indirect, often occuring, as mentioned, through portals.

Figure 2-121. King's College quad, Cambridge, England.

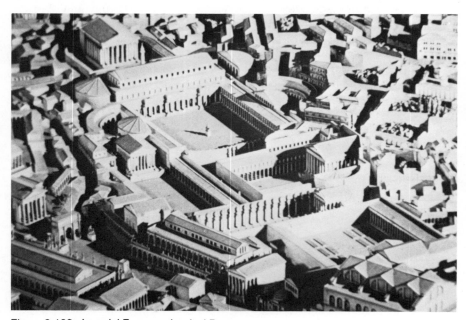

Figure 2-120. Imperial Forums, classical Rome.

Figure 2-122. Place des Vosges, Paris, France.

inverted spaces are largely isolated from the access system of the city

110

Figure 2-123. Plaza Real, Barcelona, Spain.

Figure 2-124. University of Virginia, Charlottesville, Virginia.

Figure 2-125. Place des Vosges, entrance pavillion, Paris.

they generally serve for specialized and formal uses

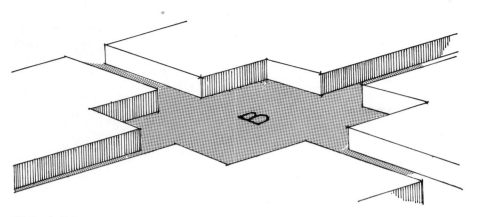

Figure 2-126.

Strategic Spaces.   At the other end of the spectrum, our second class of cluster spaces corresponds to B on our plan and to the sketch in Figure 2-126. Unlike inverted spaces, which as we have seen provide the city with formal outdoor rooms with a strong sense of enclosure, these spaces are active and central within the access system and life of the city.

Their importance and role within the urban hierarchy is a product of their direct (i.e., strategic) linkage within the urban system of linear spaces. As can be seen in the analytic sketch (Figure 2-127), the effect of openings in strategic spaces is to produce major visual breaks or leaks in the containing quality of the space percieved. This provides tension between the sense of containment and the movement which is directed away from the space through the openings. The combination of these two forces produces a very active sense of movement within the space itself, as is suggested by the ground vector in the sketch.

The scale of strategic spaces will generally determine to what extent they have the potential for supporting additional activities beyond circulation. As we will see, this also relies on the way movement is channeled through the space and how the remaining areas are treated (Component Three).

As mentioned, the importance of strategic spaces and their position or level within the urban hierarchy depends not only on their scale, but also on the number and size of linear spaces that break the containment of the defining surfaces.

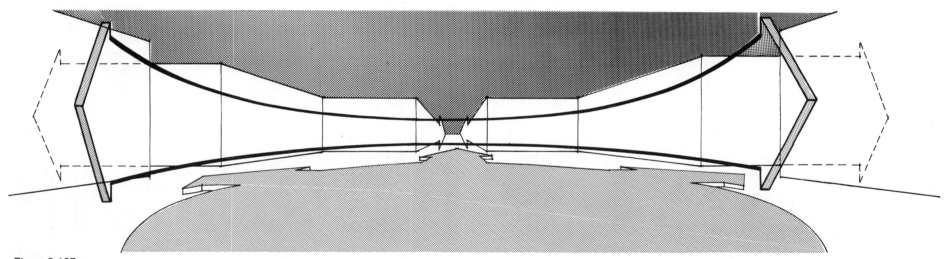

Figure 2-127.

strategic spaces are central within the access system and life of the city

When located at the crossing of major city-level linear spaces, as at the center of our plan, strategic spaces are considerably more important (and strategic) in the urban hierarchy than if located at the crossing of lower-level streets. Louisburg Square in Boston's Beacon Hill sector (Figure 2-128) is an example of a strategic square at a lower level in the hierarchy. Its primary relevance is at the sector or neighborhood level and not at the city level.

Strategic crossroads spaces when formalized have often been the basic organizational elements for entire cities. This was often true of Roman garrison towns and reemerged again in the Renaissance period. It is a distinct feature of many of the Vauban plans for the French frontier towns, as in the example of Neu Breisach (Figure 2-129), founded in 1698.

The shape of strategic spaces can also contribute to their active movement-oriented roles. The circular shapes of the Etoile in Paris, or of Finsbury Circus in London (Figure 2-130) amplify the sense of circulation and movement around these spaces.

Figure 2-129. NeuBreisach, model.

Figure 2-128. Louisburg Square, Boston, Massachusetts.

Figure 2-130. Finsbury Circus, London, England.

113

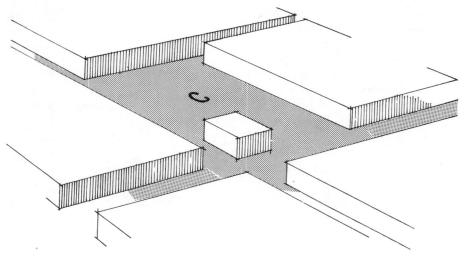

Figure 2-131.

Figure 2-132. San Giovanni e Paolo Square, Venice.

Compound Spaces. Outside of the somewhat unusual cluster spaces that come under the two headings discussed, most cluster spaces tend to be hybrids. Not being necessarily crossed by only city-level streets, many spaces retain a clear sense of containment, yet are still well linked within the city structure of access and movement. For this reason we will refer to this third class as compound spaces.

Typical examples of such spaces are San Giovanni e Paolo Square in Venice (Figure 2-132) and the central square at New York's Lincoln Center (Figure 2-133). In both cases, the squares are linked to major city-level axes on one side, while otherwise having only local links. The bridge in the Venice case is an example of this. As such they are both important city-level squares, yet still retain supportive qualities for a variety of additional uses. Rockefeller Plaza in New York is another example of such a city-level compound space. Though surrounded by sector-level streets, it is strategically linked to Fifth Avenue (with a local level pedestrian street).

Figure 2-133. Lincoln Center, New York City.

Another characteristic that often contributes to the greater supportive quality of compound squares is spatial complexity. More complicated spatial forms than the simple square, rectangular, or circular shapes seen earlier help to subdivide squares and provide subspaces that are supportive of a variety of activities. Medieval squares often have such complicated and informal shapes. Other ways in which spaces can be given more complex and supportive forms is through the use of buildings that either bridge over, as in the example of central Bergamo (Figure 2-134), or are placed within the space as in the example of the city hall in New York (Figure 2-135). In both cases, spaces are fragmented and subdivided into subspaces that can more easily support other activities. In the New York case, the city hall also acts as a major focal element. We will return to this dual effect under Component Three.[10]

Figure 2-134. Bergamo, Italy, central squares.

compound spaces combine inverted and strategic characteristics and uses

Figure 2-135. City Hall Square, New York City.

An additional technique for achieving a more complex and supportive quality in urban squares is the changing of levels. This again is a factor which, depending on the extent it is used, overlaps with Component Three elements. Major changes in levels, however, as in Rockefeller Plaza and the Spanish Stairs in Rome (Figures 2-136, 2-137), provide important subdivisions in these spaces, which to a large extent explains their highly supportive qualities.

In the earlier closed order cities of the medieval period, where the lower-level street systems prevailed, strategic squares with a high degree of enclosure were common. Because of the smaller size of incoming streets, and thus the smaller breaks in the enclosing surfaces of the space, these strategic spaces retained characteristics of inverted spaces in terms of their sense of enclosure. As such, they functioned more typically as compound spaces. While providing major focal points and crossroads in the urban access system, they were still highly supportive of a wide range of additional uses. The introduction of the automobile has, needless to say, often compromised this mixed use in modern times.

A common device used for the purpose of reducing the impact of incoming streets, mentioned earlier in conjunction with Place des Vosges, is the portal (Figure 2-125). While formalizing the entrances into a square, these have the additional benefit of strengthening the sense of containment within spaces. The Hoher Markt square in Vienna, as well as Piazza Dante in Verona and the Piazza del Duomo in Milan (Figures 2-138 to 2-140), all utilize this device.

Figure 2-136. Spanish Steps, Rome.

116

Figure 2-137. Rockefeller Plaza, New York City.

the use of level changes is a common device in the production of compound spaces

Figure 2-138. Hoher Markt, Vienna, Austria.

Figure 2-140. Galleria entrance, Piazza del Duomo, Milan, Italy.

Figure 2-139. Piazza Dante, Verona, Italy.

portals reduce the impact of incoming streets

117

Cluster Spaces within the Urban Hierarchy. Because of the importance of location and linkage of cluster spaces, in addition to their form (shape and scale), a description of their function and role within the hierarchy of the city must rely on a matrix that incorporates all of these variables.

The chart on the next two pages, utilizing the basic characteristics of shape, scale, and linkage, situates many of the squares discussed in the preceding pages relative to each other. The additional modifying impact of Component Three elements that can alter these positions are not included. Figure 2-142.

Space Chart Organization. [Note the Chart in Figure 2-141.] From top to bottom left is a range that represents the scale of spaces. This ranges from small and intimate at the top, to large and impersonal at the bottom. From top left to right is a range that represents the extent of linkage within the structure of the city. The more completely enclosed (and often more isolated) spaces are located toward the left, while spaces more heavily punctuated by incoming streets are toward the right of the chart.

The curving diagonals from top left to bottom right indicate the three classes discussed in the preceding pages. Where the scale of cluster spaces is intimate and definition is strong (toward the upper left corner), all three classes tend to share similar supportive qualities.

The height of buildings though not represented in the chart is critical to the form of spaces defined. As with linear spaces, when height to width falls below a certain ratio, a sence of spatial definition is lost, while above a certain ratio, spaces become overbearing. Again however, it is the absolute scale of the spaces relative to the human body rather than ratios per se (golden or otherwise) which provides the important use messages.

Looking briefly at some of the cluster spaces discussed in the preceeding pages, we can see that our three classes to not represent absolute divisions but broad and general ranges within which various spaces can be located. Spaces like the King's College quad in Cambridge (no. 1 and figure 2-121) and the complex of squares in Bergamo (no. 2 and figure 2-134) are intimate in scale and have limited or minor links with the surrounding cities. They are located at the upper left hand corner of the chart. Cluster spaces like P. Signoria in Florence (no. 5) and Finsbury Circus (no. 7 and figure 2-130), being larger and more strategically linked, are located in the central part of the chart. The largest spaces sit at the bottom of the chart from left to right depending on the degree of containment and the importance of the links to the city. While at the left of the chart we have the strongly defined and essentially isolated (inverted) St. Peter's square (no. 16) at the other extreme, Place de l'Etoile-Charles DeGaulle in Paris (no. 18), is strongly linked, immense in size and weak in spatial definition. More of a cluster ''pattern'' than a spatial form, it functions as an active movement-oriented space within the strategic class.

The actual role of these various spaces in the life and hierarchy of the cities is only partially represented in this chart. The uses housed in the defining buildings, the activities and elements within the spaces proper, all effect the actual importance and role of these spaces. Very large spaces, as we will see later, are often broken down in scale with the use of trees, small structures, changes in level, etc.

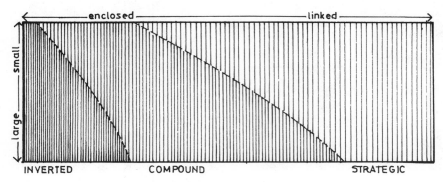

Figure 2-141. Space chart organization.

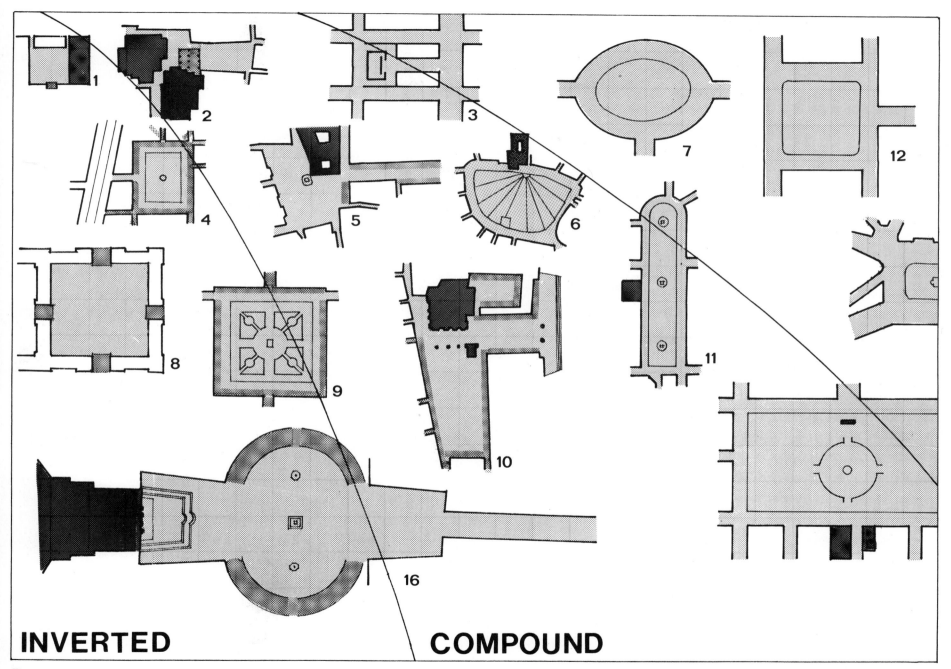

INVERTED

COMPOUND

Figure 2-142.

119

(cut page 121 along dashed line and join to plan on page 119)

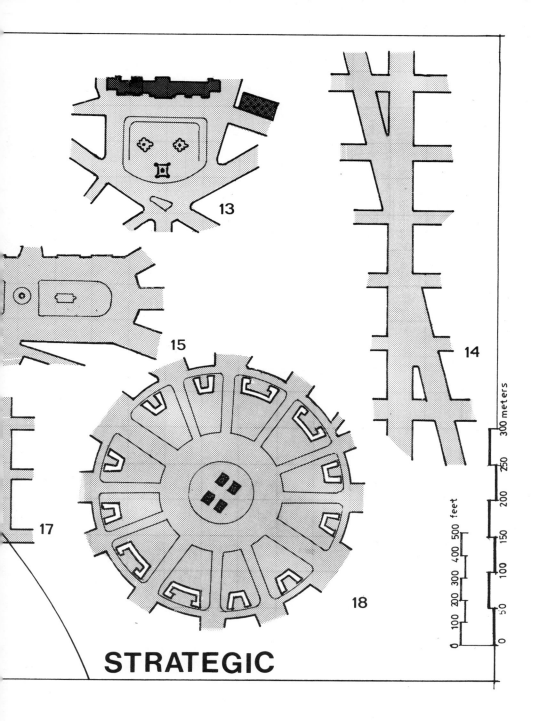

1. **King's College quad, Cambridge, England—**
   approx. 0.5 acres/0.2 hectares.
2. **Piazza del Duomo and Piazza Vecchia, Bergamo, Italy—**
   approx. 0.9 acres/0.35 hectares.
3. **Rockefeller Plaza, Rockefeller Center, New York City—**
   approx. 1.1 acres/0.45 hectares.
4. **Plaza Real, Barcelona, Spain—**
   approx. 1.3 acres/0.5 hectares.
5. **Piazza della Signoria, Florence, Italy—**
   approx. 2 acres/0.8 hectars.
6. **Piazza del Campo, Sienna, Italy—**
   approx. 3.7 acres/1.5 hectares.
7. **Finsbury Circus, London, England—**
8. **Cour Carrée, The Louvre, Paris—**
   approx. 4.25 acres/1.7 hectares
9. **Place des Vosges, Paris, France—**
   approx. 4.6 acres/1.8 hectares.
10. **St. Mark's Square and the Piazzetta, Venice, Italy—**
    approx. 4.4 acres/1.7 hectares.
11. **Piazza Navone, Rome, Italy—**
    approx. 3.5 acres/1.4 hectares.
12. **Charlotte Square, Edinburgh, Scotland—**
    approx. 4.7 acres/1.8 hectares.
13. **Trafalgar Square, London, England—**
    approx. 5.3 acres/2.1 hectares.
14. **Times Square, New York City—**
    approx. 6.5 acres/2.5 hectares.
15. **Place de la Republique, Paris, France—**
    approx. 7.5 acres/3 hectares.
16. **St. Peter's Square, Rome, Italy—**
    approx. 10 acres/4 hectares.
17. **Washington Square, New York City—**
    approx. 14 acres/5.6 hectares.
18. **Place de l'Etoile-Charles DeGaulle, Paris, France—**
    approx. 14 acres/5.6 hectares.

STRATEGIC

Scales and Systems of Linear and Cluster Spaces. Beyond the shape, scale, visual complexity and location of linear and cluster spaces and their association with urban levels, out experience of the city also relies on the inter-relationship of these spaces. In principle, when we move through the city, regardless of the mode of movement (walking, cycling, driving, etc.), we generally visualize in our minds a path or trail between our location and point of destination. This is heavily reliant on our ability to visualize, or see in our mind's eye, the relationship of the streets, squares, etc., as systems.[11]

Returning to our simple town plan (Figure 2-143), in a journey from point A to point B, we may move along portions of several classes of streets that are at different city levels as determined by the physical characteristics discussed in the preceding section. For this journey, we will rely on a series of specific left and right turns, as well as landmarks, distinctive features, and land uses. Beyond the single journey, however, the urban experience, which involves countless journeys, is based on two additional factors: the first concerns the scale of the city blocks produced by the streets, and the second concerns our ability to conceptualize the relationship of streets.

Scale of the Street Matrix. With multimodel access as a basic characteristic of the urban environment, the scale of the blocks, which is determined by the street layout, produces different scales in what can be referred to as the matrix of the access system. Referring to our plan, the matrix of the city-level system of spaces is appropriately scaled to city-level access and the use of vehicles. As we move down to the sector level, the matrix, produced by sector-level streets, is correspondingly finer. Access is geared to shorter and more frequent journeys. At the local level, where access is largely pedestrian, the scale of the matrix is finer still. It reflects and supports the much more intense human activity expected at this level of the city.

The use of super blocks in modern planning, in addition to encouraging the detachment of buildings from the public domain discussed earlier, has also tended to negate the notion of levels of activity and differences in access modes associated with matrix scales.

Geometry of the Access Plan. With regard to our experience of the city, as determined by the relationship of public spaces, the second factor concerns our ability to conceptualize the city as a plan. Beyond the question of matrix scale, this basically concerns geometry. Closely associated with the question of hierarchy, geometry provides distinct relationship qualities that facilitate our understanding of the city.

At the city level, with the use of geometry, we can easily visualize the system of both linear and cluster spaces. In our A to B journey, the more important city-level streets and squares provide a simplified system and basic reference backbone. As such, we tend to rely on this system for basic orientation and to establish our location relative to the remainder of the city. While at the city level geometry helps us to visualize the organization of the city, at the sector and local levels we also rely on relationship qualities provided by geometry as well as the memory of details. Geometry provides a reliable mechanism for predicting. While this conceptual mechanism and the notion of hierarchy were either weak or absent in the labyrinthlike medieval cities, it is to these specific devices that Renaissance city-makers turned as they sought to provide an overall sense of structural clarity and coherence in their cities.[12]

Where a combination of different ''levels'' of public spaces was superimposed as in the later Paris plan, the urban system became both highly expressive and supportive of a wide range of access modes and of urban uses in general. In this connection, it might be suggested that an excessive reliance on the rigid geometry of the gridiron, extending over large areas, was a major shortcoming of many industrial cities. Lacking variety and hierarchy, these city plans were limited in their supportive capacities. Conversely, a serious problem with many modern plans today is the lack of an easily visualizable geometrical plan. In addition, of course, most modern plans are conceived at a scale geared to car access only and are not, as such, supportive of other access modes.

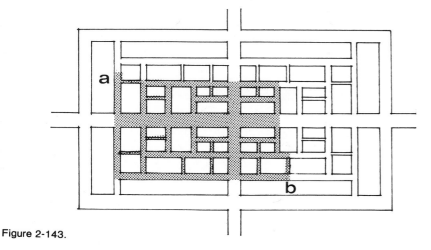

Figure 2-143.

Closed and open systems. Although the subject of urban systems lies essentially beyond the scope of this present book, one final factor should be briefly discussed. This concerns whether streets are dead-ended, producing what Christopher Alexandre has called "tree" or closed, systems, or are part of continuous "semilattice" or open systems. The first is typical of traditional "natural" cities while the second is common in modern "artificial" cities. The limiting quality of treelike systems is that they greatly reduce the choice of routes we can take from one point to another. This is illustrated in the transformation of our plan (Figure 2-144) where movement from A to B is now limited to one route only, whereas several alternatives were open before. Alexandre's argument is that this tends to segregate the city into specialized one-use areas while also greatly reducing the range of associated activities in the public domain. This is the case because associated activities, like his example of a newstand, rely on the basic multiple-access role of the street. It is the overlap and crossing of routes (of A to B journeys) that gives rise to and supports such secondary activities.

Reverting to our earlier discussion concerning the expressive and supportive quality of spaces, one can see how Alexandre's argument is in essence an extension of the basic use messages provided by spaces but within the total context of the city as a system of access.[13]

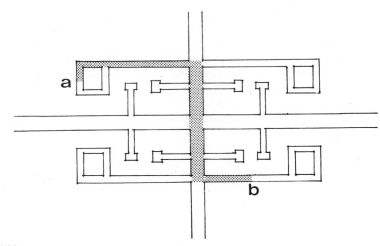

Figure 2-144.

COMPONENT TWO
THE TREATMENT OF DEFINING SURFACES

Under our second component, we focus on another vital source of information in our experience of the city, and of the public domain in particular. This component concerns how buildings, as defining surfaces for the public spaces of the city, provide additional information about the uses of individual buildings. Also important is how the interior domain that building surfaces contain (private,. semiprivate, etc.) and the exterior public domain that they create interrelate.

As mediating devices between different domains, building surfaces play a vital role in providing both expressive and supportive qualities in the urban experience. Like the walls of rooms inside buildings, the surfaces that define the spaces of the public domain strongly affect the character and quality of these spaces. Not only does the surface treatment provide various expressive qualities (through materials, textures, colors, styles, etc.), but the openings within the surfaces extend and expand the interior spaces contained and exterior spaces defined, creating both visual and functional overlap and linkage.

In the example of an apartment building by Antonio Gaudi in Barcelona (Figure 2-145), the treatment of the building surface that faces the public domain provides not only character to the space but also a wealth of information about the interior functions of the building, while also confirming the multiple role of the street it defines.

Figure 2-145. Casa Mila, Barcelona, Spain.

the surface treatment provides information about the interior function of buildings

125

WALLS AND FACADES

In our examination of building surfaces, we find that, like built and spatial forms, they are highly expressive sources of information. As mentioned earlier, surfaces can tell us about the uses of a building and how they link with the access system of the city. In this regard the treatment of surfaces (like built and spatial forms), is expressive in both functional and symbolic terms.

The primary mechanism through which functional and symbolic linkage is established between interior and exterior domains are openings—windows and doors. Windows visually extend the interior domain out and beyond the containing surfaces of buildings, while also expressing, within the public domain, the nature of the interior uses. Doors provide direct functional linkage between the two domains. In principle, we can describe a building facade as a surface which, through the use of openings, not only establishes visual and functional linkages between interior and exterior domains, but also, through their treatment, acknowledges and reinforces the special role of the public domain that they ''face.'' It is this that distinguishes a facade from a wall.[14]

If we consider specific cases, we find that in both functional and symbolic terms the absence of openings in a building surface generally suggests that its uses are either of a storage (warehousing, etc.) or exclusionary, like a defensive castle or city wall. In both cases, the basic access role of the public domain is minimal as is the secondary role of supporting the additional activities discussed earlier.

In an example of the three college buildings (Figure 2-146), three fundamentally different approaches illustrate the changes in attitude with regard to surface treatment and the changes in the role of the public domain that have occurred in the twentieth century. The building at the right in the photo (a museum) not only provides a ''Sunday-best'' use of materials and architectural detail, but also through its use of openings provides a clear statement about its interior uses. As such, it provides linkage and continuity between the two domains that acknowledge the role and value of the public space of the street.

Figure 2-146. College buildings (Yale U.) New Haven, Connecticut.

The second building, an extension of the museum, was built in the mid-fifties and is a clear product of the Modern Movement in full swing. Lacking any openings on the major street wall (which is treated in solid masonry), it effectively turns its back on the public domain it otherwise participates in defining. One might add, however, that the small setback provides an appropriate articulation with the older building as well as an indication of an entrance. The third building, an outstanding academic building by Paul Rudolf, represents the sculptural approach mentioned in Part One. Treated largely as an independant form, it establishes only weak rapport with other buildings in defining the street while attracting perhaps an undue amount of attention to itself.

a facade establishes visual and functional linkages between the public and private domains

In the next two examples (Figures 2-147, 2-148), again of academic buildings (in Oxford), the difference between the facade and the wall is clearly evident. In the first case (Figure 2-147), a subtle play on the symbolism of the city wall and the surface as a facade can be seen. While the massive qualities of stone and the use of castellations are both culturally associated with the defensive and exclusionary nature of the city wall, the surface is heavily punctured with windows and doors which expresses a strong rapport between the interior and exterior domains. This suggests that the street is considered a valid part of the city and an extension of the interior domain of the buildings. The subtlety comes in the apparent contradiction between these two aspects of the treatment, at once exlusionary and yet also establishing an active interrelationship between the private and public domains. The result is a building that expresses the notion of a somewhat autonomous (and exclusive) institution, yet which maintains a rapport with the city it participates in creating.

A second example (Figure 2-148) a modern academic building (now extended twice the length seen in the photo), has also utilized exclusionary city-wall characteristics. The virtual absence of openings, however, denies the street its varied role as a public space. This is not a facade but a wall. It is an example of how, in the modern tradition, the dualistic role of buildings, containing interior space while also defining exterior space, has often been lost. The delightful and traditional quality of Oxford, which has always relied upon and expressed a "town and gown" dialectic, is no longer apparent.

Before looking more closely at how openings function as mediating devices between domains, we will briefly consider how they affect the scale and character of the public spaces we experience.

In principle, the organization of openings in building surfaces, like the basic organization of surfaces discussed under Component One, can have the effect of modulating the scale of public spaces. Like the vertical/horizontal organization of surfaces, the organization of openings can either accelerate or retard the directional movement of the eyes while providing corresponding use messages.

the facade also provides symbolic information

Figure 2-147. Lincoln College, Oxford, England.

Figure 2-148. Kebel College, Oxford, England.

In the example of town houses facing (and defining) Washington Square in New York (Figure 2-150), the basic massing is essentially horizontal. As such, the overall surface of these buildings is formal and highly directional. The impact of openings, however, as can be seen in the analytic sketch (Figure 2-151), produces a vertical rhythm that clearly provides a counterforce to the horizontal movement. This creates a sense of scale and visual complexity more consistent with the passive quality and use of the square as a park.

The impact of openings in providing scale in the public domain is most obvious when this is combined with modulation within the facade surface itself. The case of Commonwealth Avenue (Figure 2-50) is a good example of this as is the case of terrace houses in Brighton, England (Figure 2-149).

Figure 2-150. Washington Square, New York City.

Figure 2-149. Adelaid Crescent, Brighton, England.

Figure 2-151.

THE EXPRESSIVE QUALITIES OF OPENINGS

Openings not only visually and functionally extend and link the interior and exterior domains, but they also provide us with information that makes our experience of the city meaninful. The expressive qualities of openings, as with built and spatial forms, are of both functional and symbolic origin. As such, their meaning is complex and closely associated with climatic, cultural, and social conditions of particular places and times. For this reason, what openings suggest and express about the uses inside, and the way access and linkage occurs, varies almost as much as spoken languages. These "visual codes" must be studied in each locale in order to be fully understood.

In functional terms, the sizes of openings are, as in our example of the museum building, often generally associated with the size of interior spaces as well as the nature of the uses contained there. Thus, major openings generally tend to suggest major spaces that serve for collective activities. Specialized spaces, like concert halls and theaters, which can be expressive of their functions through their forms (or Component One) are notable exceptions. Smaller openings for windows are more typically associated with smaller spaces and more intimate activities. A range of uses, retail, commercial, residential, etc., can be "read" in the facades of the buildings in Figure 2-152.

Such differences are also influenced by climatic conditions. While the use of large windows is coherent in warm and moderate climates, the need for maintaining warmth, both actual and psychological, in colder climates has traditionally limited larger windows to public and commercial uses. The case in Figure 2-152 (in Maine), is again an example of this. In the warmer climate of Spain, large expanses of glass are used throughout in another Gaudi building (Figure 2-153). This extensive use of glass would be inconsistent with the colder conditions in northern settings, a fact that escalating oil prices has emphasized in recent years.

Figure 2-152. Exchange Street, Portland, Maine

Figure 2-153. Batallo House, Barcelona, Spain.

While larger openings are generally expressive of more public uses, at the ground level, as in the examples shown, they also provide a direct visual and spatial extension of the public domain. This, in conjunction with the wide range of goods and displays that can be seen as one walks down a street, explains in part the magic and attraction of commercial areas, even when the shops are closed.

As can be seen in Figures 2-154 and 2-155, the examples on this page, the simple linearity of street spaces, when defined by surfaces with large window openings at the ground level, become visually much more complex. Like side chapels along the nave of a cathedral, each shop provides an expansion of the space into a different setting.

This spatial effect of expansion through window openings can be diagrammatically expressed as in Figure 2-156.

While the expressive qualities of all openings can be discussed in purely functional terms, their meaning also frequently relies heavily on symbolic associations.

Figure 2-154. Paris.

Figure 2-155. The Rows, Chester, Wales.

openings provide visual and spatial extensions of the public domain

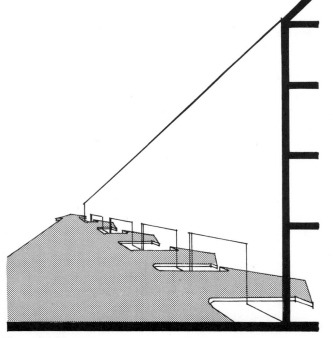

Figure 2-156.

130

In general, the size of door openings, like windows, give clues to the nature of the interior uses as well as to the extent of the linkage intended between the interior and exterior domains. The expressive qualities of doorways, however, has also historically relied on ideas and values symbolically associated with various treatments. In the example of the street in Paris (Figure 2-154), while the shop doorway has a highly transparent treatment, the heavy residential entrance to the right is clearly private and more exclusionary.

In the examples in Figures 2-157 to 2-159, the idea of a doorway as a portal is strongly associated symbolically with the historic city gate. As can be seen in the more recent examples in Figures 2-160 to 2-162, the treatment of entrances can still, within a modern idiom, express a wide range of ideas with regard to the uses contained and to the nature of the linkage. Nothing confirms or supports the use of public spaces as effectively as do entrances.

Figure 2-158. Gate pavillion, Styre, Austria.

Figure 2-157. Quirinale Palace, Rome.

Figure 2-159. Zuid residential district, Amsterdam, Holland.

131

Figure 2-160. Social services building, New York City.

Figure 2-162. Church, Greenwich Village, New York City.

Figure 2-161. Court building, New York City.

openings also rely on symbolic associations

THE INTERRELATIONSHIP OF DOMAINS

In terms of the actual implications of openings as we move through the city and seek access to people and activities, it is not only the location and treatment of openings that is important. Equally important is how the area immediately in front of facades affects the transition between the two domains.

In this regard we can identify what we will refer to as a "zone of transition" (Figure 2-163). Here, both the treatment of openings and of the space in front become vital sources of information that expresses how linkage between the exterior and interior domains is intended.

As can be seen in the following pages, many different treatments can be used to achieve this zone of transition. These various treatments express, in both functional and symbolic terms, the nature of the interrelationship between the two domains. The amount of space left between the two is clearly a major factor. The use of plantings, sunken wells, and staircases are all variations on the ancient tradition of the castle moat. They suggest and provide a buffer between the two domains, which is consistent with residential uses as well as the character and role of local residential streets. The choice and quality of treatment of the ground level of buildings, including the zone of transition if appropriate and consistent with the role of the street or cluster space faced, can add immeasurably to the expressive and supportive quality of these spaces.

Figure 2-164. Portsmouth, England.

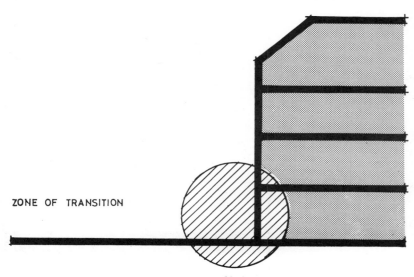

ZONE OF TRANSITION

Figure 2-163.

ground-level treatment determines the nature of the transition between the interior and exterior domains

133

Figure 2-165. Greenwich Village, New York City.

Figure 2-166. Greenwich Village, New York City.

Figure 2-169. Mykonos, Greece.

Figure 2-167. Washington Square, New York City.

Figure 2-168. Brooklyn Heights, New York City.

Figure 2-170. Brooklyn Heights, New York City.

Within central urban areas, where densities are higher, the use of the public domain is more active, intense, and less personal. It is generally more consistent for the use of the ground floor of buildings to be of a public nature and the zone of transition to be correspondingly less divisive and more active. In other words, a greater visual interest and animation is provided for the street.

In residential buildings, as in Figures 2-171 and 2-172, the public domain extends into the access system within the buildings as it becomes semiprivate. While the use of entrance canopies is both expressive and supportive of this extension and overlap of the two domains, in the remainder of the ground floor the division is smaller, less emphatic than it was in the case in the lower level, more passive streets than seen earlier. The closer residential buildings are to the commercial center of cities, the more consistent and logical, in both expressive and supportive as well as economic terms, for the ground level to be essentially public in the form of shops, restaurants, etc.

The richness of commerical areas in visual and spatial terms is often associated with the greater complexity and supportive capacity of the zone of transition. A high degree of permeability, as in the examples on this and the next page, can provide a complex three-dimensional lacework of subspaces highly supportive of a wide variety of activities.

In the example shown in Figure 2-173, the zone of transition extends below the street level, which effectively doubles its capacity.

Figure 2-172. Fifth Avenue, New York City.

Figure 2-171. Manhattan, New York City.

where a greater overlap is consistent

135

Figure 2-173. Bleecker Street, New York City.

a high degree of permeability is consistent with the role of public spaces in commercial areas

Figure 2-174. Rue de la Liberté, Dijon, France.

Figure 2-175. Place du Chatelet, Paris, France.

136

In a narrow pedestrianized street in the central sector of the town of Dijon, in France (Figure 2-174) the zones of transition on either side of the street extend far into the linear space. As such, moving along this space is virtually equivalent to moving through a linear network of small cluster spaces.

The use of cafes, as in Figure 2-175, provides an intermediate "stage," where clients are at once inside and outside, actors as well as observers. Few devices have been conceived that are more effective in populating and humanizing urban public spaces than this one.

Another important technique for producing highly supportive conditions in denser central city areas is the use of that age-old (and yet to be improved upon) device, the arcade. As in the outstanding example of this in central Bern, Switzerland (Figures 2-178 and 2-179), this provides something akin to the side aisles in cathedrals. While being an extension of the activities of the street, these pedestrian spaces are also protected. The example in Figure 2-176 is an unusual use of the arcade at the second level in the city of Chester in Northern Wales. The photo in Figure 2-177 shows the arcade around the central space at the University of Virginia, mentioned earlier. In the example of the arcade surrounding Place des Vosges in Paris (Figures 2-180 and 2-181), the spatial complexity, expressed in the accompanying analytic sketch (Figure 2-182), makes it ideal in providing this otherwise enormous and very formal square, once the setting for royal coronations, with supportive qualities it would otherwise lack.

Figure 2-178. Marktgasse, Bern, Switzerland.

Figure 2-176. Second level arcade, Chester, Wales.

Figure 2-177. University of Virginia, Charlottesville, Virginia.

Figure 2-179. Marktgasse, Bern, Switzerland.

a supportive device yet to be improved upon

Figure 2-180. Place des Vosges, Paris.

Figure 2-181. Place des Vosges, Paris.

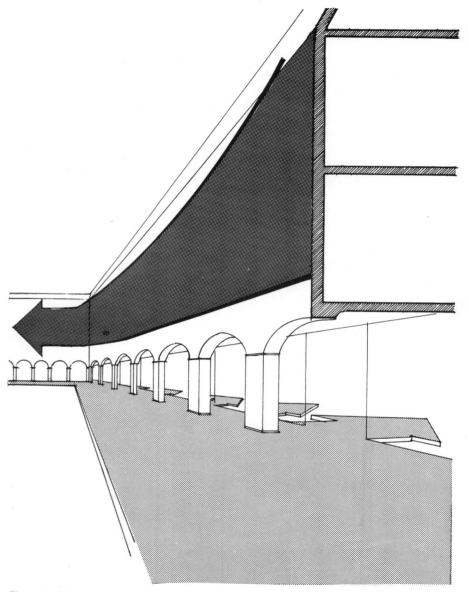

Figure 2-182.

COMPONENT THREE
GROUND TREATMENT AND FURNISHING

Like floor surfaces inside buildings, the choice and detailing of ground materials in public spaces, if consciously considered and consistent with the expressive qualities of components One and Two, can be critical factors in our experience of the public domain of the city. Areas specifically devoted to movement, as well as areas for other activities, can be made explicit. Whereas level changes can delineate and subdivide, various surface materials suggest, both in functional and symbolic terms, the kind of activities intended.

The use of various elements in the furnishing of our public spaces can also have a significant impact in the expressive and supportive qualities of the city. Again it is the consistency with the use messages provided through components One and Two that is critical. Elements like fountains, trees, etc., can structure spaces by creating focal points, while also dividing them into a variety of subspaces and activity areas.

The use of furniture, and seating in particular, largely determines to what extent the public spaces of the city can be social facilitators as opposed to merely transient spaces. Whether watching and observing the ever-changing spectacle of the city, gathering and meeting with friends and neighbors, or simply taking a break, all this is heavily reliant on and determined by how well we furnish our public spaces.

Figure 2-183. Louise Nelvelson Square, New York City.

the ground treatment and choice of furnishing is critical to the use of public spaces

GROUND TREATMENT

The Allocation of Access Areas

Being that access is a primary function of the city and that the automobile has become the dominant means of access, decisions concerning the use of public spaces are generally determined by traffic requirements. The use and treatment of nontraffic areas is frequently a secondary consideration.

Within a more holistic approach, however, wherein the expressive and supportive qualities of built and spatial forms (Component One), as well as defining surfaces (Component Two), are considered in conjunction with the overall use of public spaces, the location and channeling of movement (both vehicular and pedestrian) cannot effectively be considered independent issues.

There are some parallels in the arrangement of interior rooms that can be useful in our dealings with public spaces. Though limited to the less disruptive movements of people, the subdivision of a room through the channeling of movement can largely affect the types of uses facilitated.

In the example of a living room (Figures 2-184a and 2-184b), one can see how different arrangements can effect the subdivision and ultimate use of space. In the first case (Figure 2-184a), a typical disposition of furniture around the space provides an undifferentiated use of space that includes various movements through it. This, in principle, is not very dissimilar to early medieval squares before the advent of major vehicular traffic. In the second case (Figure 2-184b), the channeling of movement along specific paths provides for the creation of various subareas that are more specifically supportive of various uses.

In two cases of college courtyards in England (Figures 2-185 and 2-186), the use of different materials in producing areas and channeling movement provides these spaces with clearly expressive qualities. The well-manicured lawn, like carpets, delineate central areas while channeling movement around or through the spaces.

A similar flexibility in the channeling of movement in public spaces is highly relevant with regard to both pedestrian as well as vehicular traffic. The location of the latter, through or around public spaces, the number of vehicular lanes, the width of space reserved for widewalks, etc.—all these are purely questions of choice and each affects the uses possible.

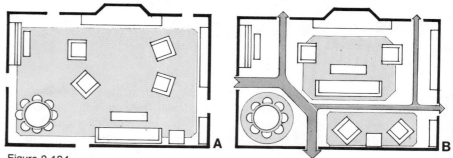

Figure 2-184.

Where the nature of the city and the urban experience are seen as directly associated with a "range" of access modes as well as a wide variety of associated activities, vehicular traffic, as opposed to the modern tradition, must, and is increasingly being put in proportion and made to coexist. In the urban context, neither the bicyclist nor the pedestrian have traditionally been second-class citizens. Rather, as earlier discussed, it is the coexistence of a multiplicity of access modes and other activities that is the hallmark of the city.

Figure 2-185. College quad, Oxford, England.

Figure 2-186. College quad, Cambridge, England.

Materials, Colors, Patterns and Level Changes

The second source of information that ground treatment provides concerns the uses suggested by the materials. This involves the choice of texture, colors, patterns and level changes.

In a living room, the use of a carpet invites and suggests certain types of activities. In public spaces, the use of grass is soft and relaxing, both to the feet and the eyes, while absorbing sound and producing natural odors. All of these sensory factors combine to suggest and support passive activities, as in Dublin's magnificent St. Stephens Green (Figure 2-187). In contrast, hard materials, depending on their texture, will generally suggest more intensive uses, as in the example of St. Mark's Square in Venice (Figure 2-188). Uses associated with various materials, however, will vary from one place and society to another as affected by climate, local traditions, etc. Thus, large cluster spaces, when exclusively treated with hard materials, may be meaningful in climates and societies where gathering is an integral characteristic of public life but often irrelevant in countries where neither the climate nor local traditions suggest it.

Since, as suggested, various materials become associated, both functionally and symbolically, with different uses, public spaces can be subdivided in an expressive manner by varying the materials.

Figure 2-188. St. Mark's Square, Venice.

Digure 2-187. St. Stephen's Green, Dublin, Ireland.

the choice of materials will suggest and support particular uses and vary from one context to another

141

In the example of a medieval street in Norwich, England (Figure 2-189), while rough stone is expressive and supportive of wheeled traffic, smooth flagstones are provided for pedestrian movement. The line of curb stones between these two acts as a retaining element that also explicitly demarks the subdivision of the ground surface. In the example in Portsmouth, New Hampshire (Figure 2-190), the use of granite (the mining of which is a regional industry), provides a highly expressive treatment for a pedestrian street crossing. It is a clear statement to the motorist that here the road is not their exclusive turf and an overlap of use occurs.

As suggested, the choice of materials and the associated uses varies from one place to another. It constitutes a "local code" that planners and designers must understand and learn to "speak" with.

A further dimension in the expressive quality of materials is added through the use of colors, patterns and level changes. Through these, not only can spaces be subdivided and earmarked for various uses as discussed above, but also they can visually modulate and organize spaces.

In the example of Sicilian Avenue in London (Figure 2-192), the vertical modulation of the space with the columns in the facades of the building is carried into the ground surface through the variation of colors and the use of a pattern. In Rome's Capitoline Hill Square (Figure 2-193), the "clustering" organization and character of the space is expressed and reinforced in the radial ground pattern. This symbolically stresses the importance of the space as a focus in the city.

Figure 2-189. Norwich, England.

materials become symbolically associated with specific uses

Figure 2-190. Portsmouth, New Hampshire.

The use of level changes can also be important in the expressive quality and use of public spaces. From a simple six-inch curb to slopes and steps, these help to organize and subdivide spaces.

In the example in Figure 2-191, the combination of street curbs, material changes, and color patterns help to differentiate areas and indicate pedestrian zones. In the following examples, while the bowl-like quality of Sienna's great Piazza del Campo is dramatized by its sloping surface (Figure 2-194), steps in Boston's Government Center Square (Figure 2-195) and a new square in Lower Manhattan (Figure 2-196) create a subspace in the first and provide a vantage place from which to stop and watch in the second.

A further dimension in the expressive quality of materials is added through the use of colors, patterns, and level changes. Through these, not only can spaces be subdivided and earmarked for various uses as discussed above, but also they can visually modulate and organize spaces.

In the example of Sicilian Avenue in London (Figure 2-192), the vertical modulation of the space with the columns in the facades of the building is carried into the ground surface through the variation of colors and the use of pattern. In Rome's Capitoline Hill Square (Figure 2-193), the "clustering" organization and character of the space is expressed and reinforced in the radial ground pattern. This symbolically stresses the importance of the space as a focus in the city.

The use of level changes can also be important in the expressive quality and use of public spaces. From a simple six-inch curb to slopes and steps, these help to organize and subdivide spaces.

Figure 2-192. Sicilian Avenue, London, England.

Figure 2-193. Campidoglio Square, Rome.

Figure 2-191. Father Demo Square, Greenwich Village, New York City.

patterns help to organize and subdivide spaces

143

Figure 2-196. Liberty Plaza, New York City.

level changes also help to organize and subdivide spaces

Figure 2-194. Piazza del Campo, Sienna, Italy.

Figure 2-195. Government Center Square, Boston, Massachusetts.

FURNISHING

In our public spaces, the elements we provide, like the furnishing inside rooms, are critical in our use of them. Both the functional and symbolic effects of furnishings in organizing and subdividing spaces, as well as in providing supports for various activities, are central to the success or failure of most public spaces.

In this section we will see how three basic categories of furnishing can serve in providing a wide variety of supportive conditions beyond the effects of ground treatment. The first of these categories concerns the use of elements that serve as focal points. Freestanding elements, such as sculpture, monuments, fountains, etc., have long been recognized as powerful organizing devices because of their high visibility. As discussed earlier, it is this visibility that also gives focal elements a high symbolic importance and which, conversely, gives symbolic importance to the spaces in which they are located.

The second category of furnishings concerns the use of space-dividing elements. Here we will consider how the use and combination of various elements helps to subdivide spaces into subspaces. This includes structures of various sizes, columns, lampposts, trees, etc.

The third, and perhaps most important category of furnishing, is seating. No less than the seating we provide in rooms, the supportive quality of public spaces is to a large extent a direct function of the quality and quantity of seating provided. Seating is the most obvious and explicit statement that the public domain is, or can be, more than merely for access and movement.

Figure 2-197. Washington Square, New York.

like within buildings, furnishing provides supports for a variety of activities

145

Focal Elements

Freestanding elements like towers in buildings (Figure 2-198) act as focal points in space. As such, they physically modify the spaces they are in by introducing points of tension which, in relationship with the containing effects of the building, have the visual effect of structuring the spaces they are in.

In Figure 2-199, which is otherwise a copy of the sketch in Figure 2-127, the addition of a monument organizes and structures the space into distinct subareas. At the base of the obelisk, a central subspace is created, while the remainder of the space now "moves around." Thus, both functionally and symbolically, the role and importance of the space as a significant position in the city has been increased. In the example of the Capitoline Hill Square in Rome discussed earlier (Figure 2-193), the equestrian statue at the center provides a strong symbolic effect while, in conjunction with the ground pattern, structuring space.

Figure 2-198. George Square, Glasgow, Scotland.

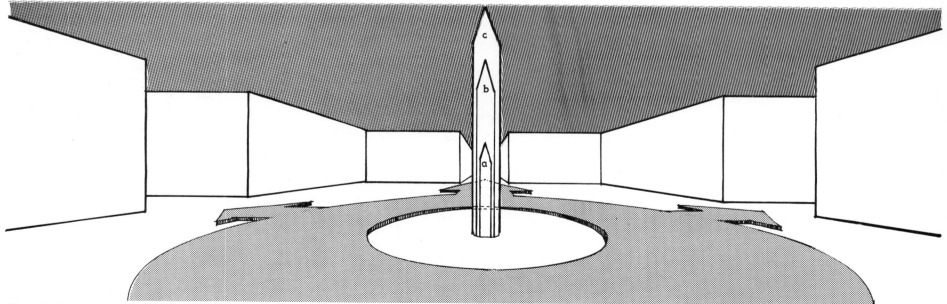

Figure 2-199.

focal elements structure spaces while symbolically increasing their importance in the city

146

The size and specific position of focal elements are critical variables in the functional and symbolic effects they produce. Modifications in the size of the obelisk, for example (a, b, c in Figure 2-199), alters the effect on the space.

In St. Peter's Square, a combination of focal elements serve to create points of tension which complement and emphasize the spatial organization of the space.

In the center of the oval space, an obelisk stops the strong linear movement (A in Figure 2-202) toward the basilica. In conjunction with the fountains on each side of the obelisk (Figure 2-203), a cross-axis (B) is created. Counteracting the dominant directional movement of A, this cross-axis produces the kind of spatial tension typical in baroque squares.

As can be seen in Figure 2-200, taken from the dome of the basilica, the use of a pattern in the ground treatment was carefully conceived so as to reinforce the organization of the space (distinct from, yet related to, the Cathedral) as well as the visual tension created by the focal elements discussed above.

Figure 2-201. St. Peter's Square, Rome.

Figure 2-200. St. Peter's Square, Rome.

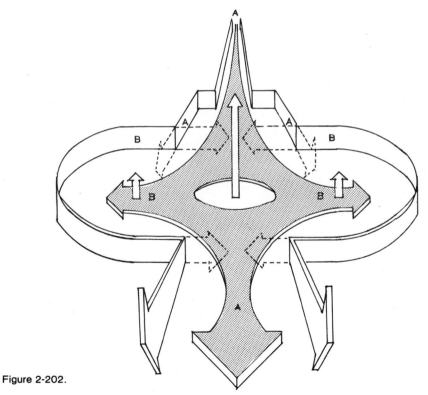

Figure 2-202.

147

Whereas building surfaces create space, focal elements, because of their high visibility, not only organize spaces, as we have seen, but also confer meaning on them. The particular power of focal elements in public spaces is that they generally incorporate symbolic associations in their own right.

It is for this reason that focal elements, whether strategically located, as are the fountains in St. Peter's Square (Figure 2-203) or quietly placed on the sidelines, as is the monument to the women of Paris in H. Bergson Square (Figure 2-204), their symbolic content contributes to the symbolic meaning of the spaces they are in. Thus, whether associated with events, values or ideas, choice and location of focal elements almost inevitably have major impacts that in meaningful city-making cannot be underestimated.

Figure 2-203. St. Peter's Square, Rome.

Figure 2-204. Henri Bergson Square, Paris.

symbolic associations of focal elements contribute to the meaning of public spaces

From Within and Beyond Cluster Spaces. Beyond the organizational and symbolic effects that focal elements have in cluster spaces, two additional effects can be observed.

The first of these concerns the role that focal elements play in providing memorable and distinct points around which people meet and gather. This function can be commonly observed in most cluster spaces with a focal element. It is particularly true where focal elements are fountains. Whether a fountain is theatrical, as in Rome's Trevi fountain (Figure 2-205), dramatic, as in St. Peter's Square, or more simple and passive, as in San Giminiano, Boston, and New York (Figures 2-206 to 2-208), as focal points fountains rarely fail to provide the city with the kind of contrast and delight upon which the quality of the urban experience relies.

The second functional effect of focal elements in cluster spaces concerns the orientational impact they have as seen from outside the space itself. The use of strategically located focal elements, a structuring concept associated largely with the Renaissance era (structured order), contributes to the visual coherence of the city.[16]

Figure 2-207. Piazza della Cisterna, San Giminiano, Italy.

Figure 2-205. Trevi Fountain, Rome.

Figure 2-206. Copley Square, Boston, Massachusetts.

Figure 2-208. Bethesda Fountain, Central Park, New York City.

The use of focal elements, when strategically located with regard to incoming streets, helps to visually link the space to the city beyond. In so doing, it further strengthens the strategic importance of the space within the larger city context while visually giving importance to the incoming streets. The effect of this is to strengthen the visual and functional hierarchy of the city.

When streets are visually linked to focal elements, as in the example of the Champs Elysees (Figure 2-212) (which is focused on the triumphal arch at the Place de l'Etoile in Paris), they become stronger orientational spaces in the urban hierarchy. The impact of the arch within the structure and hierarchy of Paris can be seen in the plan in Figure 2-211. The city level within the hierarchy of the city is based on major cluster spaces linked by major linear spaces. The scale of the arch, as can be seen in Figure 2-210, is conceived to dramatize the importance of this, the most symbolically important street in Paris.

The arch at the terminus of New York's Fifth Avenue (at Washington Square), on a more modest scale is clearly similar in effect to the Paris arch (Figure 2-209).

Figure 2-209. Washington Square, New York City.

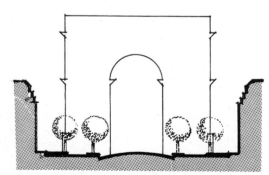

Figure 2-210. Champs Elyseé, section, Paris.

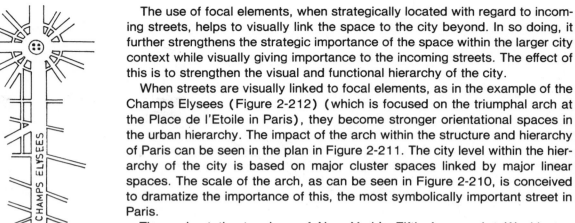

Figure 2-211.

Figure 2-212. Champs Elyseé, Paris.

focal elements strengthen the structure and hierarchy of the city

Figure 2-213. Monument Circle, Indianapolis, Indiana.

Figure 2-214. Place des Victoires, Paris.

Figure 2-215. Victor Emmanuel Galleria, Milan, Italy.

Based on similar structuring principles, a monument in Indianapolis, Indiana (Figure 2-213), helps to anchor a highly strategic space to the city-level system of streets.

As suggested, the structuring impact of focal elements is also a function of the location of the spaces they are in, with regard to the urban structure and the hierarchy. As such, when located at a more local level, as in the case of Place des Victoires in Paris (Figure 2-214), or in conjunction with Milan's famous Victor Emmanuel arcade (Figure 2-215), the impact is more localized. An exception to this is when focal elements are immense, as with the campanile tower in St. Mark's Square (Figures 2-216, 2-217). In this case, as with the tower in Florence (Figures 2-218 and 2-219), or indeed any building perceived as a tower, such as the World Trade Towers, seen in Figure 2-209, they provide orientation even if not directly associated with the street system.

providing orientational features at various urban levels

Figure 2-216. Grand Canal, Venice.

Figure 2-217. Venice.

Figure 2-218. Uffizi Galleria, Florence.

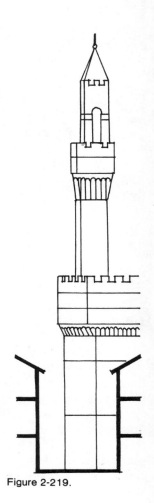

Figure 2-219.

Space-Dividing Elements

Elements within public spaces are aften less important in creating focal points than in subdividing spaces into subareas and subspaces. The relationship of two or more elements, like columns or lampposts, can produce this effect. In the Piazzetta, that portion of St. Mark's Square that extends and opens out to the sea (Figure 2-220), the use of two columns provides an edge to the space while also giving the space a symbolic gateway.

In the more ordinary circumstances of a linear space, such as the Via delle Conciliazione leading to St. Peter's Square (Figure 2-221), the linear disposition of street lamps act as unifying elements while providing modulation and a sense of progression as one moves along the space. An additional effect that such linear arrangements have is to visually subdivide the space. This will be further discussed in conjunction with the use of trees, where the effect is similar.

Figure 2-221. Via della Conciliazione, Rome.

Figure 2-220. Piazzetta, Venice.

elements help to subdivide spaces

Freestanding buildings within cluster spaces (as discussed in conjunction with compound spaces earlier), or within linear spaces, often play the double role of acting as focal elements and, because of their size, also acting as space-dividing elements. This was the case with New York City Hall, seen earlier (Figure 2-135), and buildings within the central square in Whitney, such as the pavillion known as the buttercross (Figures 2-222 and 2-223). The glass flower shop in Boston's Quincy market is a modern example (Figure 2-224).

The old chapel in the central square in the Roosevelt Island development was clearly retained, within the new space planned around it, with the double role of acting as a focal element and as a space-dividing element (Figure 1-110).

In the example of a tower in the Irish town of Youghal (Figure 2-225) the effect, as shown in Figure 2-226, is not only to provide a focal point but also to subdivide the street. Thus the street is given spatial characteristics that are static and of the cluster type.

Smaller structures and temporary elements are critical in the subdivision and "adaptation" of large public spaces to the scale of human beings and to a variety of daily activities. Among others, these elements include stands and kiosks, bus shelters, umbrellas, and parked cars.

Figure 2-223. City Hall, New York.

Figure 2-222. Market Square, Whitney, England.

buildings can act as both focal and space-dividing elements

Figure 2-224. Flower shop, Quincy Market, Boston, Massachusetts.

Figure 2-225. Youghal, Ireland.

Figure 2-226.

155

Figure 2-227. Djamaa Fna Square, Marrakech, Morocco.

Figure 2-228. Greenwich Village, New York City.

Figure 2-229. Greenwich Village, New York City.

156

Figure 2-230. Greenwich Village, New York City.

Figure 2-231. Rue St. Antoine, Paris.

Figure 2-232. Urbino, Italy.

temporary structures are useful in the adaptation of spaces for various uses

Figure 2-233. Congress Street, Portland, Maine.

Figure 2-235. Cafe pavillion, Washington, D.C.

Figure 2-234. The Tower Wharf, London.

Figure 2-236. Rockefeller Plaza, New York City (photo by Jerry Spearman).

Figure 2-237. Washington Street, Boston, Massachusetts.

In the central market place in Marrakech, Morocco (Figure 2-227), the basic definition of the space relies less on major building surfaces than it does on small-scale structures. The use of moveable stands, tents and canopies is generally comparable to the buildings in creating the complexity of spatial conditions found here.

The use of small and temporaty structures, as well as parked cars, in the Marrakech square and in examples in New York (Figures 2-228 to 2-230), can be seen as playing an important role in the subdivision of space and the provision of supportive conditions. The use of umbrellas and umbrellalike structures, as in Paris and Urbino streets (Figures 2-231, 2-232), and in other examples (Figures 2-233 to 2-236), are flexible, inexpensive, and effective devices.

There are many additional devices that are effective in the subdivision of space. These can be described as hybrids of the ones mentioned in the preceding examples.

Freestanding glass arcades, as in the superb examples in Boston (Figure 2-237), and Allentown, Penn. (Figure 2-238), produce extended zones of transition. They provide protection from the elements while giving these streets visual cohesion, complexity, and interest, highly supportive of the commercial roles they have. Variations on the arcade as a space-dividing element can be seen in the examples in Figures 2-239 and 2-240.

Figure 2-238. Allentown, Pennsylvania.

providing visual cohesion, complexity, and interest as well as supportive quality

159

Figure 2-239. Inner Harbor, Baltimore, Maryland.

Figure 2-241. Nathan Philips' square, Toronto, Canada.

In Toronto's city hall square (Figure 2-241 and 2-111 a,b), the use of three arches acts as both a sculptural feature in the space while also, because of their gathering form, producing a subspace that is a reflection pool in summer and a skating rink in winter. This device is simple, elegant, and very effective.

Figure 2-240. Residential court yard, New York City.

other hybrid devices are effective in the subdivision of public spaces

The Use of Trees.   Trees can be very important elements in both the creation and the subdivision of public spaces (Figure 2-242). With regard to the second quality, the alignment of trees can have an analogous effect to the use of lampposts. This effect is clearly evident in another section of the Parisien rue St. Antoine (Figure 2-243), seen earlier (Figure 2-81). Though the scale of this major street ranks it as a city-level space, the use of trees effectively subdivides it into various use zones. The scale of the subspaces used as sidewalks are well suited for their pedestrian activities.

Beyond subdividing spaces horizontally, trees can also subdivide vertically. Because of the varying density of their foliage, trees can act as permeable masses that either enclose a space with a leafy ceiling, as in the cases seen earlier (Figures 2-64 to 2-66) or, as in Figure 2-244, can fragment a space with a semitransparent lacework. The effect of trees as space-creating and space-dividing elements is further illustrated in Figure 2-246.[17]

Figure 2-243. Rue St. Antoine, Paris.

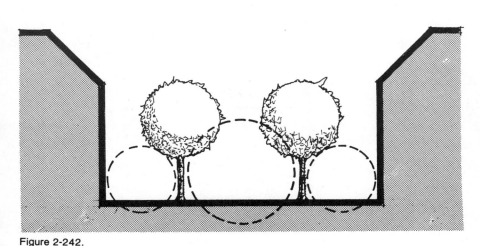
Figure 2-242.

trees can completely change the scale of spaces

Figure 2-244. Greenwich Village, New York City.

161

Figure 2-245. Brooklyn Heights, New York City.

Figure 2-246.

Trees Within Cluster Spaces. The use of trees within cluster spaces can often be more critical than in linear spaces. Since an important function of cluster spaces is often to provide conditions that are supportive of a variety of activities, the space-defining and dividing effects of trees can often be basic form-making elements. In cases where spatial definition is weak (Figure 2-247), or where the buildings are too high, as in the case in New York's Lower Manhattan district (Figure 2-248), trees can create or significantly modify spaces.

This effect can also be seen in an example in Heidelberg (Figure 2-249), where a few trees clearly modify the scale of the space perceived. The scale of larger cluster spaces, such as Washington Square in New York (Figure 2-250), can be dramatically modified.

In cluster spaces that are specifically used as parks and where the scale is enormous, as with New York's Central Park (Figures 2-251, 252, 253), one can only loosely refer to these as cluster spaces since they are never seen as spatially defined forms. Rather, they might be described as constituting a preurban or natural category of space. This of course is one reason why they provide a sense of releif within the city.

Figure 2-247. Sheridan Square, New York City.   Figure 2-248. Abingdon Square, New York City.

Figure 2-249. Heidelberg, Germany.

Figure 2-250. Washington Square, New York City.

163

Figure 2-251. Central Park, New York City.

Figure 2-253. Central Park, New York City.

Figure 2-252. Central Park, New York City.

in parks, trees recreate a natural order of space

Seating

Seating, although somewhat less prominent in visually subdividing spaces, is nonetheless very effective in creating subareas and in giving public spaces a critical supportive role in the life of the city. As with rooms inside buildings, public spaces often become places to stop only when seating is provided.

Through the disposition of seating, both cluster and linear spaces can be given the supportive capacity for more passive activities. When placed immediately adjacent to buildings and extended into spaces, as in sidewalk cafes, the supportive transition zone becomes a prominent part of the space itself. Cases in Williamsburg, Virginia, and St. Mark's Square (Figures 2-254 and 2-255) are good examples of this.

Within active and strategic spaces where traffic movement accounts for a major function of the space, as in Figures 2-256 to 2-258, seating provides the critical supports for the more passive activities otherwise impossible.

The character, location, and arrangement of seating are of critical importance as is the relationship to the other activities in the space. Just as important as the disposition of seating in rooms, the disposition of seating in public spaces cannot be considered in isolation.

As with any artifact, the form of seating is expressive of functional intention. Whereas rigid and formal seats may be less inviting, more contoured and flexible seats invite longer stays. The same applies to the disposition and arrangement of seats. Locations and patterns can invite the solitary spectator or groupings of people.

Figure 2-255. St. Mark's Square, Venice.

seating gives public spaces a critical supportive role otherwise impossible

Figure 2-254. Williamsburg, Virginia.

165

Figure 2-256. Central Square, Piraeus, Greece.

Figure 2-257. Lincoln Square, New York City.

Figure 2-258. Avenue of the Americas, New York City.

the character, location and arrangement of seating is of critical importance

In the following examples the organization of seating can make the user a spectator on the sidelines, as in a local square in Algeciras, Spain (Figure 2-259), or an active part of the action as in an otherwise marginal space in Midtown Manhattan (Figure 2-260). The use of seating in linear spaces, as on Sixth Avenue in New York (Figure 2-261), can add an important social role to such spaces.

Whether added to spaces or built into the landscaping, as in Figures 2-262 to 2-267, if, as was suggested in Part One, seeing and being seen are among the important and enjoyable aspects of the urban (and human) experience, then seating must be considered as a major factor in the city-making process.[18]

Figure 2-260. Exxon Park, New York City.

Figure 2-259. Algeciras, Spain.

Figure 2-261. Avenue of the Americas, New York City.

167

Figure 2-262. Mykonos, Greece.

whether added to spaces or built into the landscape

Figure 2-263. Damrosch Park, Lincoln Center, New York City

Figure 2-264. Soho, New York City.

Figure 2-265. Washington Square, New York City.

Figure 2-266. Coenties Slip, New York City.

Figure 2-267. Damrosch Park, Lincoln Center, New York City

seating must be considered as a major factor in the city-making process

Notes and References—PART TWO

1. Geoffrey Scott, *The Architecture of Humanism* (first published by Constable & Co. Ltd., London, 1914, and now published by Methuen & Co. Ltd., London). This is an excellent introduction to the psychology of forms and spaces. An older and still excellent introduction is *Experiencing Architecture* by Steen Eiler Resmussen (MIT Press, Cambridge, 1964). Rudolf Arnheim's *The Dynamics of Architectural Form* (University of California Press, Berkeley, 1977) is a highly recommended reference on which many basic principles of perception in our discussion here are reliant.

2. This notion that all human activities, constructions, etc. operate as forms of communication which are in many ways analogous to languages, is in part based on the work of the anthropologist Claude Levi-Strauss and the linguist Ferdinand de Saussure. In essence what Levi-Strauss demonstrated is that basic cultural phenomena such as kindship, myth, and totemism are analogous in their organization to languages in order to make the relations between people intelligible. His most important work on this "structural" quality of cultural phenomena appeared in *the Savage Mind* (Weidenfeld & Nicolson, London, 1966). His work forms the basis for what is known as Structuralism.

   The important contribution of Ferdinand de Saussure (in *Cours de linguistic general*), on which Levi-Strauss's theories heavily rely, concern the fact that there is a distinction between words (the signifiers) and the things they represent (the signified), and that the relationship between these is socially determined and therefore essentially arbitrary. The more recent application of these principles in the analysis of man made objects is known as semiotics. In essence, this concerns the fact that every object in culture is endowed with meaning. Photography, cinema, clothing, architecture, etc., are in effect forms of communication which operate according to complex codes which are unwritten and untaught.

   This book is only loosely based on the general principles in structuralism and semiotics for which some references are provided below. The more conventional differentiation between what constitutes signs and symbols used here is not fully consistent with that in semiotics. It is more closely related to the one provided by the influential aesthetician Susan Langer in *Philosophy in a New Key: A study in the symbolism of reason, rite and art* (Mentor Books, New York, 1948). Here she suggests that "a sign indicates the existence—past, present, or future—of a thing, event or condition. The use of symbols, unlike signs are not proxy for their objects (events, conditions, etc.) but, vehicles for the conception of objects." Whereas signs are directly linked to and indicative of a state of being, symbols refer to ideas which society chooses to associate with a particular form. This is the distinction between signs and symbols that Rudolf Arnheim also utilizes.

3. The confusion that arbitrariness in architectural forms causes for the user as he tries to decode forms, is something which has received increasing attention in recent times. It is on this question that Manfredo Tafuri has focused in his book *Theories and History of Architecture* (Harper and Row, New York, 1980). The importance of understanding the relationship between forms and particular meanings in people's understanding and use of the built environment is an essential factor in making cities meaningful.

4. This is referring to the work of Wolfgang Kohler and the school of gestalt psychology in which the fact that we tend to respond, not to individual stimuli, but to specific groupings and patterns was first investigated (*Gestalt Psychology*, Livernight Pub. Corp., 1947.

   Work in structural anthropology mentioned earlier in note 2, is in some ways related to this type of analysis. According to Claude Levi-Strauss, as explained by C. R. Badcock in *Levi-Strauss Structuralism and Sociological Theory* (Hutchinson, London, 1975), "the collective aspect of cultural phenomena is to be explained by reference to the fact that all men have similar minds, at least as far as structure is concerned and hence collective

aspects of culture reflect the broadly similar mass of individual psyches." In other words, "the human nature to which cultural codes reduce and on which they are based is ultimately the nature of the mind itself." (p. 98)

5. Christian Norberg Schulz, *Existence Space and Architecture* (Praeger, New York, 1971); Kevin Lynch, *The Image of the City* (MIT Press, Cambridge, 1960). Both of these books remain basic milestones in the development of more analytic approaches to understanding the nature of human response to the built environment.

6. Maurice Merleau-Ponty, *The Phenomenology of Perception* (Routledge & Kegan Paul, New York, 1962). This book remains an excellent introduction to a descriptive approach to perception. As opposed to the more systematic causal approach in behavioral research, phenomenology is fundamentally descriptive. It does not seek to identify causes but rather the laws and principles that affect what and why we see. In essence, it maintains that what we see is never finally constituted, but constantly changing as a product of our own inner drives, needs, and basic life intentions which are forever exploring and developing. It is an approach to perception and human reality, not as mechanistic, but as dynamic and growth oriented.

7. The use of such controls in recent years so as to provide spatial definition, as well as better light exposure, coherence, and quality in public spaces is exemplified in an English publication which has been very influential in that country in recent years, *A Design Guide for Residential Areas*, produced by the Essex County Council planning department. Clearly aimed at reducing the anonymous and spaceless character of suburban developments, this guide is largely focused on how streets can be given more meaningful and supportive qualities.

   Efforts at coordinating planning and design in New York in recent years are in part associated with the early work of the Urban Design Group. Starting in the late 60's this division of the New York City Planning Department attempted to develop design controls by working directly with developers, offering incentives in terms of permitted built space in exchange for public amenities. Some of this work, including the Broadway case, was summarized in Jonathan Barnet's *Urban Design and Public Policy* (Praeger, New York, 1969). Later revisions in the New York City planning code, have focused specifically on such controls, as well as on the question of the treatment and furnishing of public spaces.

8. An application of this in more recent developments is the "S" shaped Main Street in the Roosevelt Island case seen in figures 1-110 to 116. Through the length of this street, the spatial enclosure is consistent with the active social role envisioned for it as a focus of community life. The concentration of social and commercial uses along this space is thus consistent with the form. Rather closely reproducing the traditional mixed use qualities which have always been basic to life in New York, its intended role as the focus of community life has been very successful.

   With regards to the central square (Figure 1-116), however, the result has been less successful. Other than the chapel and a corner restaurant, no other public uses have been located around the space to ensure its role, and the treatment of the space itself, as analysed in Part Three (Figure 3-82), is more reflective of mediterranean gathering cultures than of that in New York. This is an example of a form that is not consistently supported with planning and landscaping choices constituting the content.

   Gordon Cullen's *Townscape*, first published by Reinhold in 1961, reamins a basic and essential reference for anyone interested in city making and the impact which form has in people's experience.

9. The movement of the eyes as we visually explore the environment referred to as scanning has been observed and recorded in laboratory situations. The visual complexity of a space, and the effect that it has, is a product of both the quantity and predictability of these ele-

ments. The interest that a street has visually as such determines to what extent our attention is held. Where visual information is limited or redundant (predictable or "overcoded"), our involvement is minimal and the dominant "use message" is that of rapid movement.

10. In his book *Town and Square,* Paul Zucker has provided a wider classicision of squares, which the threefold classification used in this text is in some ways a simplified version of. The class referred to here as compound corresponds roughly to his "grouped squares" in his examination of Medieval squares. An earlier classic work on the shape and relationship of squares within the context of cities is Camillo Sitte's *City Planning According to Artistic Principles* first published in 1889. More recent discussions on the design of squares are the work of Rob Krier in his proposals for the city of Stuttgart presented in his book *Urban Spaces* (Rizzoli, New York, 1979).

11. In an approach to the city as a language, one could say that the individual spaces, linear and cluster, constitute the words while the interrelationship of spaces within a system and hierarchy—or plan—constitutes the stringing together of words into sentences. As such, every city provides a complex three dimensional matrix within which every town trail is but one part of the total story. Investigations into the experience of the city at this level in which time and movement are involved remains limited. Kevin Lynch's *The Image of the City* remains a basic. Additional references include *Mental Maps* by Peter Gould and Rodney White (Penguin Books, 1974) and *Environmental Knowing* by Gary Moore and Reginald Golledge (Dowden, Hutchinson and Ross, 1976).

12. The development of city-level linear spaces as basic structuring elements in the Renaissance period has been analyzed by Edmund Bacon in his book *The Design of Cities* (Thames and Hudson, London, 1967). He shows how the introduction of major streets directly linking the important squares and churches of Rome in the sixteenth century provided a "city-wide design structure." This principle, which was subsequently developed as a basic characteristic of Renaissance planning, forms the basis of what was earlier referred to as the "structured order." The introduction of a major city-level street leading to St. Peter's Square in the twentieth century (Figure 2-221) can be seen as an extension of the city-level system to this otherwise inverted space.

13. Christopher Alexandre, "The City is not a Tree" (*Design,* No. 206, February 1966). In this seminal article, Alexandre was concerned with identifying the most basic underlying principle which gives life to cities. The tendency to group similar activities together into sets and then to string them together along a centralized treelike access system, he argued, prevents the overlapping of elements and thus the creation of subsets (which involve combinations of different elements). The semilattice structure in which streets form a continuous access system, allows for the overlap of movement of town trails—and thus of subsets. He argues that "though the tree system satisfies the planner's desire for neatness, order and control, the lack of structural complexity is what is crippling our conception of the city." Alexandre also suggests that the neighborhood community as a one use and isolated set has little social or functional reality today and that as such the restrictions of the tree system are incoherent with the ways society actually works.

14. An interesting collection of studies of the way building forms and surface treatments provide important symbolic information within more primative societies is in the book *Shelter, Sign and Symbol,* edited by Paul Oliver (Barrie & Jenkins, London, 1975). In his introduction, Oliver discusses how aspects of buildings, including their siting, often represent the transformation of signs into symbols. The use of mark stones and the location of places of worship on ley-lines for example, often became symbolically important. Oliver suggests that "this is a progression from the functional to the symbolic, and it seems possible that some sites had secular and practical beginnings as signs whose symbolic attributes eventually led to their being venerated." Similar processes of transformation from sign to symbol in the treatment of building surfaces are examined in various case studies.

15. In his book *Art and Revolution* (Penguin Books, New York, 1969) concerning the role of the artist in Russia, John Berger suggests that "a sculpture appears to be totally opposed to the space that surrounds it. Its frontiers with that space are definitive. Its only function is to use space in such a way that it confers meaning upon it. It does not move or become relative. In every way possible it emphasizes its own finiteness. And by so doing it invokes the notion of infinity and challenges it. We, perceiving this total opposition between the sculpture and the surrounding space, translate its promise into terms of time. It will stand against time as it stands against space" (p. 74).

16. The effect of focal elements (monuments, fountains, etc.) within squares is also discussed in the aforementioned books by Sitte and Bacon. In Renaissance planning, starting in Rome, the strategic location of obelisk so as to be visible from outside squares as one approached them on the new city-level streets emerged as another formal principle. In this connection Bacon suggests that "the movement system emerges as a total design idea, symbolized by the obelisks positioned at its terminal points" (p. 123)

17. The importance of trees as design elements, in the sense that they can have a major impact on the character of urban spaces, is not very widely recognized outside of the landscape profession. Yet even the most elementary analysis demonstrates the major spatial impact which trees have. A recent book on the subject is Henry Arnold's *Trees in Urban Design* (Van Nostrand Reinhold, New York, 1980).

18. The importance of how seating is distributed in public spaces is in part related to the early work of E. T. Hall in "proxemics" in which he demonstrated that the way people relate and use space is deeply rooted in our culture. (*The Hidden Dimension,* Doubleday, New York, 1966). In this connection work by psychologists like Robert Sommer in *Tight Spaces* (Prentice-Hall, 1974) uses analytic techniques to determine how the distribution of furniture in various institutional settings affects use and human interaction. In a recent book by William Whyte (*The Social Life of Small Urban Spaces,* The Conservation Foundation, Washington, D.C., 1980), several plazas in midtown Manhattan have been analyzed with the aim of identifying possible relationships between intensity of use and physical characteristics within exterior public spaces. Conclusions concerning seating and other amenities have been incorporated into the New York City zoning code.

The use of time lapse photography and systematic observational techniques as used by Whyte can be very helpful in identifying how physical characteristics such as seating effects the use of public spaces. It is important, however, not to overlook the basic limitations of this kind of physical determinism for the prediction of human behavior. People's use of the city is also affected by cultural and social as well as psychological factors, and in the final analysis, none of these by themselves or even their combination can really provide a realiable prediction tool.

ADDITIONAL RELATED REFERENCES (PART TWO)

Alexandre, Christopher. *A Pattern Language.* Oxford University Press, New Yokr, Oxford, 1977.

Appleyard, Donald and Tunnard, Christopher. *The View From The Road.* MIT Press, Cambridge, 1964.

Arnheim, Rudolf. *Visual Thinking.* University of California Press, Berkeley, 1969.

Ashcraft, Normand and Scheflen, Albert. *People Space.* Doubleday, New York, 1976.

Ashihara, Yoshinobu. *Exterior Design in Architecture.* Van Nostrand Reinhold, New York, 1970.

Bachelard, Gaston. *The Poetics of Space.* The Orion Press, New York, 1964.

Barber, Paul J. and Legge, David. *Perception and Information.* Methue & Co., London, 1969.

Beard, Ruth M. *An Outline of Piaget's Developmental Psychology.* Routledge & Kegan Paul, London, 1969.

Bell, Gwen and Tyrahitt, Jacqueline (eds.) *Human Identity in the Urban Environment.* Penguin Books, New York, 1972.

Boudon, Philip. *Lived-in Architecture, Le Corbusier's Pessao Revisited.* MIT Press, Cambridge, 1972.

————. *Sur l'espace architectural.* Dunod, Paris, 1974.

Broadbent, Geoffrey. *Design in Architecture: architecture and the human sciences.* John Wiley & Sons, New York, 1973.

Broadbent, Geoffrey and Bunt, Richard and Jencks, Charles (eds). *Signs, symbols, and architecture.* Wiley, New York, 1980.

Canter, David. *Psychology for Architects.* Applied Science Pub. Ltd., London, 1974.

Charbonnier, G. *Conversations with Claude Levi-Strauss.* Cope Editions, London, 1969.

Chermayeff, Serge and Alexendre, Christopher. *Community and Privacy, Towards a New Architecture of Humanism.* Doubleday, New York, 1963.

————. *Shape of a Community.* Penguin Books, New York, 1971.

Ching, Francis D. K. *Architecture: Form, Space, and Order.* Van Nostrand Reinhold, New York, 1979.

Clay, Grady. *Close-up, How to Read the American City.* Praeger Pub., New Yokr, 1973.

Collins, George and Christiane. *Camillo Sitte and the Birth of Modern City Planning.* Random House, London, 1965.

Culler, Jonathan. *Saussure.* Fontana / Collins, Glasgow, 1976.

Ehrmann, Jacques. *Structuralism.* Anchor Books, New York, 1970.

Goffman, Erving. *Behavior in Public Spaces.* The Free Press, New York, 1963.

Guiraud, Pierre. *Semiology.* Routledge & Kegan Paul, London, 1975.

Halprin, Lawrence. *Cities.* Reinhold, New York, 1963.

Harvey, David. *Social Justice and the City.* Edward Arnold, London, 1973.

Heckscher, August. *Open Spaces, The Life of American Cities.* Harper & Row, New York, 1977.

Husserl, Edmund. *Phenomenology and the Crisis of Philosophy.* Harper Torch Books, New York, 1965.

Jencks, Charles and Baird, George (eds). *Meaning in Architecture.* Barrie and Jenkins, London, 1969.

Jung, Carl (ed). *Man and His Symbols.* Aldus Books, London, 1964.

Langer, Susanne K. *Mind: An Essay on Human Feeling.* John Hopkins Press, Baltimore, 1967.

————. *Feeling and Form.* Routledge & Kegan Paul, London, 1975.

Ledrut, Raymond. *Les Images de la ville.* Editions Anthropos, Paris, 1973.

Lee, Terence. *Psychology and the Environment.* Methuen, London, 1976.

Maslow, Abraham. *The Psychology of Science.* Henry Regnery, Co., Chigago, 1966.

Mercer, Charles. *Living in Cities; Psychology and the Urban Environment.* Penguin Books, New York, 1975.

Merleau-Ponty, Maurice. *The Structure of Behavior.* Beacon Press, Boston, 1963.

Moles, Abraham and Rohmar, Elizabeth. *Psychologie de l'espace.* Casterman, Belgium, 1972.

Moore, Gary and Golledge, Reginald. *Environmental Knowing.* Dowden, Hutchinson and Ross, 1976.

Mundle, C. W. K. *Perception: Facts and Theories.* Oxford University Press, 1971.

Newman, Oscar. *Defensible Space, People and Design in the Violent City.* Architectural Press, London, 1972.

Norberg-Schulz. *Meaning in Western Architecture.* Studio Vista, London, 1963.

Piaget, Jean. *Main Trends in Psychology.* George Allen & Unwin, London, 1970.

————. *Le Structuralism.* Presses Universitaires de France, Paris, 1972.

————. *The Psychology of Intelligence.* Routledge & Kegan Paul, London, 1950.

————. *The Mechanisms of Perception.* Routledge & Kegan Paul, London, 1950.

Powers, William. *Behavior: The Control of Perception.* Wildwood House, London, 1974.

Rapoport, Amos. *House Form and Culture.* Prentice-Hall, New Jersey, 1969.

Rapoport, Anatol. *Conflict in Man-made Environment.* Penguin Books, New York, 1974.

Rimbert, Sylvie. *Les Paysages Urbains.* Armand Odin, Paris, 1973.

Shotter, John. *Images of Man in Psychological Research.* Methuen, London, 1977.

Sommer, Robert. *Tight Spaces: Hard Architecture and How to Use it.* Prentice-Hall, New Jersey, 1974.

Webb, Eugene. *Unobstrusive Measures.* Rand McNally, New York, 1971.

Worskett, Roy. *The Character of Towns.* Architectural Press, London, 1969.

Zevi, Bruno. *Architecture and Space.* Horizon Press, New York, 1957.

PART THREE

COMPONENT ANALYSIS AND APPLICATION TO CASE STUDIES

In this part of our examination of the experience of the public domain of the city, we will utilize our three components in the analysis of existing situations wherein the visual expressive characteristics are in some ways confusing and the supportive qualities are correspondingly often weak. Because the experience of the visual environment is the product of several variables, the use of the three components can only provide us with a general starting point. The meaning that the public domain of the city has, as discussed earlier, is affected by a variety of interrelated determinants both acquired and innate. For this reason, a thorough understanding of what individual spaces mean in the general experience of people necessarily requires a detailed knowledge of the specific social and cultural context of each locale. As has been discussed, the interrelationship of form and content must at all times remain a central feature of any meaningful analysis.

In the various analyses on the following pages, a variety of typical situations are subdivided under our three component headings focusing on the major, though often not the only, source of difficulty. Often a lack of consistency between the components and their messages lies at the root of the problems. These analyses are presented in brief outline form and should only be seen as indicative rather than definitive and complete statements.

In section two, the analytic process is reversed in three case-study applications. Here the three components are used in the planning and design of typical urban developments. While the first case, a local street, is purely demonstrative and not context specific, the second, a city center, and third, a college campus, are based on specific situations and in each case follow a general programming and use analysis.

SECTION ONE
ANALYSIS OF EXISTING DEVELOPMENTS

COMPONENT ONE, BUILT AND SPATIAL FORMS

In Part One we saw that in the development of meaningful and supportive public domain in the city, the separation of architectural design from the city-planning process has frequently been a major factor in the fragmentation and deterioration of the city as a system of meaningful spaces. Although "form follows function" was a popular idiom associated with the Modern Movement, very often buildings have been conceived in terms of aesthetic effects and symbolic associations with ideas of modernity rather than their impact on our understanding and use of the city.

In this connection the notion of building forms as conventions associated with specific uses, or as typologies, has often been confused or lost. The isolation of architecture from the total context has frequently meant that the definition of the public domain as a system of spaces capable of supporting a variety of uses has also been lost.

The two examples of government-built housing in New York and Amsterdam (Figures 3-1, 3-2), while providing a sense of openness, in many ways typify the two limitations mentioned above. While the cubistic and anonymous forms are neither functionally nor symbolically indicative of the kind of uses they contain, they have the further limitations of not being indicative of how the spaces around them were intended for use. There is a distinct lack of differentiation and meaning in both the buildings and the space around.

In the following analysis, shortcomings can be seen as related to confusion in the expressive qualities of built forms, building relationships, and spatial forms, as well as to the lack of linkage between spaces and the urban systems. Additional problems can be seen as associated with questions of scale and organization of defining surfaces.

Figure 3-1. Public housing, New York City.

Figure 3-2. Public housing, Amsterdam, Holland.

the expressive qualitities of built forms

Figure 3-3. Office building, Hartford, Connecticut.

Figure 3-4. Office building, Stamford, Connecticut.

Figure 3-5. Office buildings, Indianapolis, Indiana.

ANALYSIS

In examples of modern office buildings in Hartford and Stamford, Connecticut (Figures 3-3, 3-4), and Indianapolis (Figure 3-5), like many of the buildings shown at the start of Part One, the relationship of form to interior function has been largely subordinated to exterior aesthetics. While creating visual impacts and perhaps new symbols, references to any known building type or "typology" has been obscured.

In the case of a public high school in New York (Figure 3-6), a strong reliance on forms suggestive of and symbolically associated with fortress architecture is at least confusing. One might say that it provides limited and misleading clues as to the actual use of the building.

Figure 3-6. Public school, New York City.

the expressive qualities of building relationships

Figure 3-8. Residential development, Cosham, England.

Figure 3-7. West End redevelopment, Boston, Massachusetts.

Figure 3-9. Residential development, Portsmouth, England.

ANALYSIS

In typical examples of urban renewal and development, as in Boston (Figure 3-7), Cosham, England (Figure 3-8), and in the center of Portsmouth, also in England (Figure 3-9), the relationship of freestanding buildings, towers, slab blocks, etc., by and large signify nothing. No meaningful patterns are produced in either the siting or interrelationship of these buildings. While the use of towers is essentially gratuitous and in no way associated with focal areas or activities within the developments, there is a total lack of continuity between the buildings as surfaces in terms of spatial definition.

The local road in the Cosham case, for example, is in no way suggested by the loose relationship of the buildings, and as such is not supportive of any uses other than car access permitted by the paving. It does not provide a common space for this development, which remains a collection of unrelated fragments.

the expressive qualities of spatial forms

Figure 3-10. Broad Street, Philadelphia, Pennsylvania.

Figure 3-13. Central square, Valingby, Sweden.

Figure 3-11. Central square, Rabat new town, Morocco.

Figure 3-12. Central square, Rabat.

ANALYSIS

Within many existing older cities, as seen in Part One, spatial form has deteriorated as buildings have been demolished and plots have been turned into parking lots. This is the case in the example in central Philadelphia (Figure 3-10), where the spatial form of the street has been largely lost. In the various examples of new town developments (Figures 3-11 to 3-13), expressive and supportive qualities are again weak and for essentially the same reasons as in the preceding examples.

In essence, the space-defining capacity of buildings is either lacking or the definition of space is very limited as in the cases in Rabat, Morocco (Figures 3-11, 3-12), and Valingby in Sweden (Figure 3-13). In each of these examples, spaces intended to serve as central squares and gathering places lack the spatial qualities that are either expressive or supportive of these social functions. In the case in Sweden, one can also question whether such major exterior spaces are consistent with the traditions and climatic conditions of such a northern context?

Figure 3-14. Residential development, Hartford suburbs, Connecticut.

Figure 3-15. Basildon new town, England.

Figure 3-16. Basildon new town, England.

Figure 3-17. Basildon new town, England.

ANALYSIS

In examples of new residential developments in the United States (a residential community on the outskirts of Hartford, Connecticut, Figure 3-14) and England (Basildon new town, Figures 3-15 to 3-17), while more conventional building types and architectural symbolism has been utilized, the relationship of buildings still make only vague references to the intended use of exterior spaces. Both cluster spaces (Figures 3-15, 3-17) and linear spaces (Figures 3-14, 3-16) remain only suggested.

While the social use of these spaces was at least intended in the cluster spaces, their generally unsupportive character has made them more devisive than unifying.

The use of town houses as a traditional urban form, in there cases, suggests images of the traditional village. One might ask, however, whether this is not form without content?

Figure 3-18. Empire State Plaza, Albany, New York.

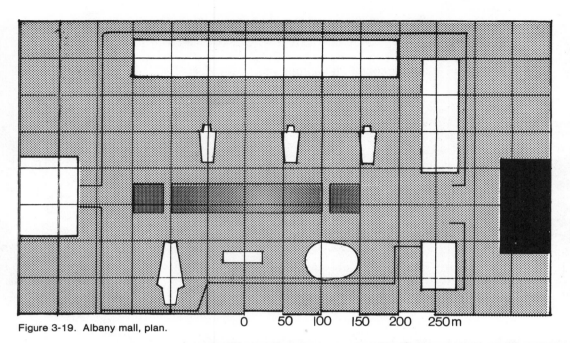

Figure 3-19. Albany mall, plan.

Figure 3-20. La Defense, office center, Paris.

Figure 3-21. Christian Science center, Boston, Massachusetts.

ANALYSIS

In the development of a new government center for the state of New York in Albany seen earlier (Figures 1-43 to 1-45), the intentions were clearly those of providing strong symbolic images (Figures 3-18, 3-19). When measured in terms of the supportive quality of the city, however, one might question whether the symbolic intentions have not been achieved at the expense of a supportive role.

Similar limitations exist in the examples of the new office center on the outskirts of Paris seen earlier La Defense (Figures 1-40, 3-20), and the new and otherwise elegant Christian Science center in Boston (Figure 3-21). Although none of these are without some positive qualities, it seems clear that the symbolic impact has in all three cases emerged as being more important than the use value they might have for the city dweller.

180

Figure 3-22. Residential towers, Greenwich Village, New York City.

Figure 3-24. Copley Square, Boston, Massachusetts.

the use of towers   Figure 3-23. Beacon Hill, Boston, Massachusetts.

ANALYSIS

As with the preceding examples in renewal areas, in new towns and new centers, the use of towers within existing urban situations can often be visually confusing. Of particular concern is the impact towers can have on the scale and character of existing townscapes and neighborhoods.

Cases of residential towers in New York's Greenwich Village (Figure 3-22) and of office towers adjacent to Boston's Beacon Hill neighborhood (Fig. 3-23), show how such structures can affect both the homogeneous quality as well as spatial coherence of existing neighborhoods. In the Greenwich Village case, the symbolic association of towers with the concept of center is in this situation inconsistent with the actual function. In the case of the office tower at Boston's Copley Square (Figure 3-24), the effect is that of overwhelming the scale of both the historic landmark church by Richardson and the space of the square itself.

Figure 3-25.

Figure 3-26.

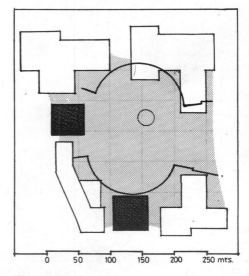

Figure 3-27.

Figure 3-28.

World Trade Center,
New York City

ANALYSIS

In the case of New York's "bigger than ever" World Trade Center many of the formal limitations mentioned in the preceding examples can also be seen.

In addition to the distinct feelings of insecurity experienced by many people standing at the base of 110-story towers (Figure 3-25), the otherwise well-defined space is immense in scale (Figure 3-26). Indeed the giant oval of St. Peter's Square in Rome, which functions as the symbolic center of a world religion, could fit inside this space as could eight football fields—and with room to spare! (See Figure 3-27.)

Additional probable sources of difficulty in the supportive character of this space concern the choice of uses at the ground level of the various buildings as well as weakness in the linkage of the space with the city. As with the Albany mall and the Parisien center, La Defense, while massive yawning lobbies occupy ground floors, commercial activities have been essentially located beneath the deck and out of sight. Another difficulty, as with the other decks mentioned, concerns the linkage of the space with the surrounding network of the city. Though one clear link with the existing street system is provided to the east, other links are minor and problematic as in Figure 3-28. As such, the space remains essentially isolated and without the activities or special symbolic role which would give it meaning.

the question of scale

Figure 3-29. Market Street, Philadelphia, Pennsylvania.

Figure 3-30. Avenue of the Americas, New York City.

ANALYSIS

In Part Two, it was suggested that the scale of defined spaces is essentially measured relative to the human body. In this regard, a space can be alienating when its size is either horizontally or vertically excessive.

In the examples of streets in Philadelphia (Figure 3-29), and New York (Figures 3-30 and 3-31), the human scale is dwarfed to the point of insignificance. While often dramatic, such spaces are frequently experienced as overwhelming canyons, ill suited to the comfort of pedestrians.

Additional shortcomings often associated with such conditions are essentially climatic in nature. Besides often being cut off from the sun, such major spaces frequently function as wind tunnels in cold seasons. As such, they produce negative microclimates rather than the protective microclimates more typically associated with cities.

Figure 3-31. Amsterdam Avenue, New York City.

Figure 3-32.

Government Center, Boston, Massachusetts

Figure 3-33.

ANALYSIS

The problems of scale are very often related to ground area, or the horizontal dimensions, rather than to the height of surrounding buildings.

In the example of Boston's Government Center (Figures 3-33, 3-34), while the space is centrally located and well linked into the urban system, the actual size of the space is extremely large. As can be seen in Figure 3-32, St. Mark's Square and Barcelona's Plaza Real could fit in the main space while Bath's Royal Circus and Sienna's Piazza del Campo could all be neatly tucked behind. Though providing exposure for the impressive city hall building, the scale of the square makes its use as a popular space at best difficult. This situation is particularly aggravated during the long (cold and windy) winter months, since no supportive microclimate is produced by the surrounding buildings.

Figure 3-34.

Figure 3-35. Dilworth Plaza (Penn Square), Philadelphia, Pennsylvania.

Figure 3-36. Citicorp Plaza, Lexington Avenue, New York City.

ANALYSIS

In the use of sunken plazas, the question of linkage is frequently a major problem. The examples on this page all remain largely detached from surrounding movement patterns. In spite of providing access to subway stations and lower-level entrances the cases in Philadelphia (Figure 3-35) and New York (Figures 3-36 to 3-38) remain largely detached from the major activity level of the city.

Because of the difficulty of linking sunken plazas with the surrounding urban system, their use relies heavily on the introduction of special activities within them. While the well-known sunken plaza at Rockefeller Center in New York provides a crowd-drawing skating rink in the winter time, its success as noted earlier also relies heavily on the use of many different levels between the street and the lower area.

Associated shortcomings of sunken plazas concern the discomfort experienced by many people at being in an "observed" rather than "observer" position. While this provides extroverts in the Rockerfeller Plaza skating rink a welcomed opportunity for display, other more passive uses like cafes succeed only when hidden underneath umbrellas, which one might argue, largely defeats the natural exhibitionist quality of sunken spaces.

Figure 3-37.

Figure 3-38.

Figure 3-39. Residence for elderly, New York City.

Figure 3-40. College residence, Cambridge, England.

Figure 3-41. College building, New York City.

ANALYSIS

As suggested in Part Two, the organization of defining surfaces affects the scale of urban spaces in terms of the suggested mode and speed of movement.

In the examples this is particularly critical in that each of these spaces are local streets serving a range of activities and movements. The strong dominance of horizontal organization of these facades in New York (Figures 3-39, 3-41) and Cambridge, England (Figure 3-40) can be seen to accelerate the sense of movement while conversely negating the more intimate scale associated with the pedestrian experience. A vertical fragmentation of these buildings would have provided both a better fit with existing buildings as well as the greater visual complexity associated with the mixed use of these urban spaces.

186

COMPONENT TWO, THE TREATMENT OF DEFINING SURFACES

As with Component One, when focusing on the urban experience, the treatment of defining surfaces cannot be considered independently of the uses that the buildings contain or that the public spaces are intended to serve. The interrelationship and coherence of these in our experience is critical. While the forms of buildings and spaces provides the basic context, the treatment of defining surfaces establishes the relationship between the activities contained within buildings and the public domain. The *consistency* between this treatment and the specific use of the spaces contained in buildings as well as the spaces defined in the public domain is basic to the character and use of both. This concerns not only the expressive quality of materials, detailing, etc., but also the use of openings (windows and doors) and the zone of transition at the ground level.

In the preceding three examples (Figures 3-39 to 3-41), as well as the two cases shown in Figures 3-42 and 3-43, spaces are clearly defined by buildings, but the lack of active ground-level uses within the buildings, for whatever reasons, is clearly a denial of the multiple role of the public domain. The deadening effect a lack of mixed uses can have is evident in London's South Bank arts center (Figure 3-43). It is an example of how form and content, insofar as the quality and use of the public domain is concerned, cannot be considered independently.

In following examples, while buildings generally define the public domain in terms of basic massing, there is a lack of differentiation between walls and facades. Following these, other examples focus on the question of openings and zones of transition. As discussed it is not only the expressive quality of the treatment that is essential but also the consistency with the specific nature of the public spaces defined at various urban levels.

Figure 3-42. Central square, La Grande Borne, France.

Figure 3-43. South Bank art center, London.

differentiation between walls and facades

Figure 3-44. Town houses, Philadelphia, Pennsylvania.

Figure 3-46. Medical center, Richmond, Virginia.

Figure 3-45. Infill houses, Oxford, England.

Figure 3-47.

Figure 3-48.

ANALYSIS

The question of whether a defining surface is perceived as a facade, acknowledging and "plugging into" the public domain, or as a wall, denying and effectively negating it, has become an increasingly important source of difficulty in much modern architecture.

Limitations can be seen as associated with a failure to clearly adopt a "language" of facade. While in the case of town houses in Philadelphia (Figure 3-44), which provide an exclusionary fortress wall-like treatment, new houses in a local street in Oxford (Figure 3-45) expose what are in effect party walls to street side (though facades are seen when coming from the opposite direction).

The use of translucent and mirror glass, which has been fashionable in recent times, while occasionally providing interesting reflections of neighboring buildings, as in examples in Richmond, Virginia (Figure 3-46), Boston (Figure 3-47), in effect function as solid walls rather than facades. Though possibly acceptable as a "one of" within an existing urban context, the total absence of any human references in this type of anonymous treatment limits the contribution to the urban environment and experience. Its use is particularly problematic at the ground level of buildings, where the reflection of oneself can hardly be described as an expansive experience or a source of useful information. The wall/facade question is often a particular problem with megastructure developments, as in an example in Brooklyn (Figure 3-48), where the character of the existing street is completely denied.

the treatment of openings

Figure 3-49. Central square, La Grande Borne, France.

Figure 3-50. Residential court, La Grande Borne, France.

Figure 3-51. New Square, Portland, Maine.

Figure 3-52. Office building, Philadelphia, Pennsylvania.

ANALYSIS

The importance of openings in the confirmation and animation of public spaces is dramatized in the following examples.

In the case of the development in Figures 3-49, 3-50 (on the outskirts of Paris), attempts at reducing the deadness of windowless walls has relied on the use of painted murals, while in Philadelphia (Figure 3-51) the anonymity of a glass tower is hidden behind the ghostlike remains of an earlier (and richer) era.

Perhaps a more telling example of the importance of openings in the defining surfaces of urban spaces is the case of a new square in the city of Portland, Maine (Figure 3-52). Here, the exposed party wall, resulting from the demolition of a corner building (to make for the square in question) has been disguised with a painted facade. Ground-level shop windows (also painted), clearly admit the importance of such activities in association with a cluster space. No doubt actual windows and entrances opening onto real activities would contribute to the greater success of this space, which has remained little used though strategically located.

Figure 3-53. Basildon new town, England.

Figure 3-54. Local street, Oxford, England.

Figure 3-55. Residential development, Amsterdam, Holland.

Figure 3-56. Suburban development, Boston region, Massachusetts.

ANALYSIS

Particular difficulties associated with the typical examples on this page concern the ground-level treatment and the ''zones of transition.''

In the example of a local-level linear space in England's Basildon new town (Figure 3-53), which is a pedestrian-only access space, ambiguity in the role of the space results from the contradictory treatment of entrances and transition zones on the two sides. While primary entrances, complete with mailboxes and semiprivate setback courts, occur on the right, the left side is defined with backyard fences and gates that function as service entrances only.

In Oxford (Figure 3-54), Amsterdam (Figure 3-55), and in a residential suburb of Boston (Figure 3-56), similar ambiguities occur. In each of these cases, the role of the linear access spaces remains ambiguous and marginal due largely to either the absence of entrances or the contradiction discussed in our first example. Transition zones that remain unclear as to purpose or ownership further add to the confusion. An additional problem in the case of the Oxford street (which is common in much redevelopment work today), is that, although the space ''reads'' as a through street, it has in fact been turned into a dead-end street. As such, though expressive of a public role, in reality it functions as a semiprivate access-only space in which the nonresident is eyed with question and suspicion. One might suggest that it is a dubious privatization of the public domain.

COMPONENT THREE, GROUND TREATMENT AND FURNISHING

Under our third component, the treatment of ground surfaces and the furnishing of public spaces clearly becomes inseparable from the questions of planning and traffic management. The extent to which traffic is allowed to dominate public spaces and the degree of mixed access which is permitted are clearly fundamental factors in the multiple supportive role of public spaces. As discussed in Part Two, the choice of materials to express both movement and other activities, as well as the choice and arrangement of furnishings, can be critical in the expressive and supportive qualities of public spaces.

In the case of Times Square in New York (Figure 3-57), which is a major strategic space in the city, the overwhelming dominance of traffic movement makes the wider use of this space very difficult. Pedestrian space is restricted to narrow sidewalk edges and minute, almost inaccessible central islands. A similar limitation can be seen in London's Piccadilly Square. At the other extreme, many new spaces such as one in Lower Manhattan (Figure 3-58), are totally segregated from any access routes. As such, their role becomes equally limited within the life of the city. In this case the potential use of the space (which is sixty feet above the street) is also limited by the lack of supportive treatment and furnishing. Very little reason is provided for anyone to go literally out of their way to come to this space. In the following pages we will consider limitations related to the choice of uses and the location of movement, choice of ground materials, and the use of furnishing, including the location and relationship of seating.

Figure 3-57. Times Square, New York City.

Figure 3-58. Chemical Bank building plaza, New York City.

the choice of uses

Figure 3-59. Place de la Liberation, Dijon, France.

Figure 3-60. Grande Place, Arras, France.

Figure 3-61. Notre Dame Square, Paris.

ANALYSIS

The choice of uses permitted in public spaces, as discussed, is firstly a question of planning rather than form. In the examples on this page, ambiguity and contradictions result in the relationship of use choices with the spatial form of the spaces.

In the case of two cluster spaces in France, Place de la Liberation in Dijon (Figure 3-59), and the Grande Place in Arras (Figure 3-60), though each is well defined and suggestive of important roles within the structure of these cities, their use has been for the most part relegated to the mundane storage of vehicles.

In the case of the newly created square in front of Notre Dame Cathedral in Paris (Figure 3-61), the hard surface suggests that it is intended for major public gatherings. Lacking supportive activities around (like shops, cafes, etc.) and virtually devoid of any furnishings within, it remains an underutilized and at best symbolic space, though located in the very heart of the city.

Figure 3-62.

Figure 3-63.

Grand Army Plaza, New York City

Figure 3-64.

ANALYSIS

The location of traffic channels through cluster spaces is often the "kiss of death." In the case of New York's Plaza square its location at the crossing of two major city-level streets makes it an important strategic space in the city structure. The basic use of this space as a traffic circle, however, seriously limits its potential as perhaps one of the most important focal spaces in the city.

Elimination of the traffic loop through the northwestern portion, as well as the reduction of the little-used street in front of the Plaza Hotel (bottom left in Figure 3-62), would greatly improve the potential use of this space. Further measures might include the replacement of the meaningless neoclassic landscaping (Figure 3-63) with more supportive ground treatment, along with more useful seating and perhaps a few kiosks and a cafe. At the present, activity in this space relies heavily on intinerant street entertainers and vendors, both of these at last being encouraged by the city rather than seen as obstructions.

Figure 3-65. Sergelsgatan Street, Stockholm, Sweden.

Figure 3-66. Prudential center, Boston, Massachusetts.

ANALYSIS

Beyond the questions of traffic channeling and choice of other uses, the choice of ground treatment and materials can play key roles in the expressive quality of public spaces. In order for these choices to be meaningful, however, they must be carefully considered and holistically linked with the other two components.

In the examples in Figures 3-65 to 3-70, the dominant impression, which at least this writer has, is that ground treatment and the choice of materials has been largely limited to a decorative role.

In cases in Stockholm (Figure 3-65) and Boston's Back Bay (Figure 3-66), though colorful patterns and materials might be said to add visual interest to these pedestrian spaces, the relationship to actual uses (or intended uses) is marginal or dubious.

Figure 3-67. Time-Life Plaza, Avenue of the Americas, New York City.

Figure 3-68. Sergel Square, Stockholm, Sweden.

Figure 3-69. Evry new town, France.

Figure 3-70. Greenwich Village, New York City.

ANALYSIS

Similar to the preceding cases, the examples in Figures 3-67 to 3-70 can all be seen to suffer from a degree of arbitrariness.

The spaces created through the setback of towers on New York's Avenue of the Americas (Figure 3-67), though often treated with expensive materials, often lack the qualities that would allow them to function as the kind of public spaces intended in the zoning legislature that led to their creation. In most cases (and with the help of decorative fountains), they subsequently tend to function as visual setbacks for the towers behind rather than as meaningful public spaces.

In the examples of Sergel Square in Stockholm (Figure 3-68), an elevated deck in the new town of Evry in France (Figure 3-69), and at the base of the residential towers in Greenwich Village discussed earlier (Figures 3-22 and 3-70) the use of textures and colorful patterns, while again visually decorative, doesn't in fact "mean" anything insofar as the actual use of these spaces is concerned. These can be described as further examples of form without meaningful content.

Figure 3-71. Paternoster Square, London.

Figure 3-72. Central square, Skarholmen, Sweden.

Figure 3-73. Thamesmead, new town, England.

ANALYSIS

In many of the cases in the preceding analysis, the lack of furnishing has also been a limitation. In the examples on this and the following pages, it can be seen as a central shortcoming.

In cases in London (Figure 3-71), Skarholmen, Sweden (Figure 3-72) and the English new town of Thamesmead (Figure 3-73), the use of hard surfaces, typical of those in many Mediterranean countries, underlines the potential difficulty of transplanting solutions from one culture and climatic setting to another. Though the weakness or absence of furnishing in warm "gathering" societies might not be a serious problem, in northern nongathering climates and societies such spaces are often problematic. The success of cluster spaces in northern countries seems generally more dependent on a smaller scale, a heavier concentration of supportive furnishing, more organized activities, and strong linkage to access routes.

In the case of the London development (which is adjacent to St. Paul's Cathedral in the heart of the city), the lack of sufficient supportive furnishing and related activities has only further served to emphasize the dubious relevance of this type of space in a city where summer and fine weather are more often in the domain of dreams than reality.

Figure 3-74. University of Essex, Colchester, England.

Figure 3-75. University of Essex.

Figure 3-76. Waterside residences, New York City.

Figure 3-77. Commercial road, Portsmouth, England.

ANALYSIS

Similar to the preceding examples, the use of large concrete decks as squares at the University of Essex on the outskirts of Colchester, England (Figures 3-74, 3-75), is again of questionable relevance in this notoriously rainy country. But for one cafeteria, cluster space-related activities like shops, cafes, etc., are lacking while student residence halls have been stacked in dubious tower forms detached from the center. While these are also questions of land-use choices, the limitations of the spatial forms of the squares, in terms of the role they play, is further aggravated by the virtual absence of any furnishing. Similar limitations can be seen in the plaza of a new development in New York City (Figure 3-76).

Another example underlines the potential problems associated with the current fashion of pedestrianizing major ''city-level'' streets (Figure 3-77). Immense in scale, a central street in Portsmouth, England (one of two so treated), fills up only on Saturdays, which is the traditional shopping day in England. Outside this period, however, in spite of some furnishing (trees, a fountain, some seating, etc.), these pedestrianized spaces remain nearly empty. Incoherent with the suggested use messages suggested by the scale of these spaces (which were conceived for major traffic movement), Portsmouth can be said to have lost its traditional multipurpose main street.

the significance of focal elements

Figure 3-78. Springfield, Massachusetts.

Figure 3-80. Penn Square, Philadelphia, Pennsylvania.

Figure 3-79. Marine Midland Plaza, New York City.

Figure 3-81. Olympic Village, Munich, Germany.

ANALYSIS

The relevance of sculpture as focal points in public spaces is invariably associated with the significance that these elements have for people. In this connection, highly abstract pieces, as in the examples in Springfield, Massachusetts, in Figure 3-78 (which also doubles as an elevator), and in New York (Figure 3-79), although providing visual organization and interest within these spaces, they fail to provide meaningful associations for most people.

In the examples of sculptural elements in Philadelphia (Figure 3-80), and at a residential development outside Munich (associated with the Olympic Games) (Figure 3-81), a megaclothespin and the use of sewage pipes as sculptural elements, while perhaps less abstract and more amusing, are not more likely to provide strong emotional attachments than the previous examples.

The choice of art pieces in public spaces is admittedly a highly debatable issue. But as with built and spatial forms, the question of meaning cannot be disregarded if the experience of the city is given a central position in the city-making process.

and the use of seating

Figure 3-82. Central Square, Roosevelt Island, New York City.

Figure 2-83. Wall Street plaza, New York City.

Figure 3-84. Chase Manhattan Plaza, New York City.

ANALYSIS

Of all the forms of furnishings, seating is unquestionably the most basic and essential to the varied supportive role of the city. Surprisingly, however, in many modern developments, seating is conspicuous only by its absence.

In the various examples in New York City, the almost total absence of seating, as in many of the cases on the preceding pages, gives the impression of a house before anyone has moved in. Although these cluster spaces, in principle, suggest the possibilities associated with rooms, lacking the necessary supportive furnishing their use is largely limited to through movement.

Such limitations are particularly regrettable in New York, where an enormous office work force seeks relief during midday lunch breaks. In a new plaza in Lower Manhattan (Figure 3-83), a few unplanned edges represent the sum total of seating in the space. Though a bit more generous, the otherwise elegant Chase Manhattan Plaza (Figure 3-84) in this respect is still underfurnished. In the case of Roosevelt Island, the central space seen earlier (Figure 1-110) is limited in use at least in part due to the limited amount of furnishings (Figure 3-82).

199

Figure 3-85. Walnut Street, Philadelphia, Pennsylvania.

Figure 3-86. Osborn Road, Portsmouth, England.

Figure 3-87. Freiburg, Germany.

ANALYSIS

In these final examples we come full circle in the interrelated constellation of urban components. What is emphasized in these three situations, in Philadelphia (Figure 3-85), Portsmouth, England (Figure 3-86), and Freiburg, Germany (Figure 3-87), is the necessity of considering the use of seating within the total context of architectural and spatial design as well as land-use planning and sociocultural needs and traditions.

As in a room, the location of furniture within the total context of a space, of the movement areas, and of associated activities is essential. Observation confirms that people love to sit and observe the urban phenomena or gather and become an active part of it. Neither, however, will occur just anywhere even when seating is provided. The disposition and arrangement of seating must be based on an understanding of what seating means to people and of how they actually use it. Dropped in the middle of large spaces, as in these examples, the would-be user is put in a highly conspicuous and, relative to the total space very uncomfortable position. Not surprisingly, the seating in each of these cases has not contributed very much to the use of the spaces.

SECTION TWO
APPLICATION TO CASE STUDIES

In this final section, the aim is that of demonstrating how, when the experience of the public domain is given a central position within the city-making process, form and content must be *simultaneously* considered. The cases provided on the following pages are presented as demonstrations of this principle rather than as models for universal application. As has been suggested, the actions of people in the public domain cannot be easily explained (or predicted) in simple causal terms. Rather one must look to basic human needs and intentions. This is related to physiological and psychological as well as social and cultural factors and as such is changeable. Patterns of behavior having both universal as well as localized characteristics can be identified only to a limited extent. Ultimately, analysis of what physical conditions mean in terms of actual use must be considered on a case by case basis and rely on extensive and systematic observation as well as other techniques. In the planning and design of new developments, clues should be sought within the given culture, while an incremental and experimental development process can allow adjustment over time. In this connection, degrees of incompletion in new developments can allow for the input and participation of people as local communities develop.

CASE STUDY 1: A LOCAL STREET

Within the urban context, one of the most important public spaces affecting the daily lives of people is the street on which they live. Quantitatively it represents the bulk of the public domain.

It is the first extension of the private domain and a primary determinant of people's access and linkage (as well as relationship) with their immediate neighbors and the larger city beyond. The form that this vital part of the public domain takes is thus critical in people's experience of the city.

In this first case study our three components are utilized to help focus the development process on a local residential street. Within a simple city plan that relies on a repetitive and easily understood geometry, through-access, essential to the basic role of the public domain, is maintained (Figure 3-88). Relying on the principles of space and use-messages developed under Component One, modifications in the layout of the street and of the individual housing units provide a scale and visual complexity in the spatial form consistent with the local character and function of the street. On the following pages the use of the three components in the production of this local (sector-level) street is detailed.

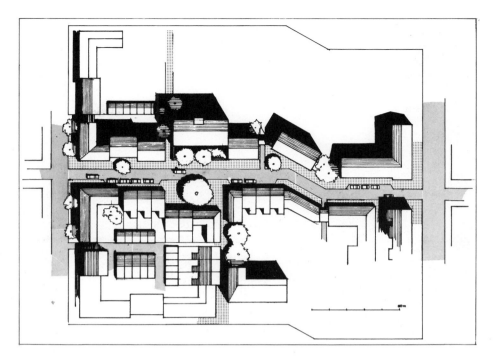

Figure 3-88.

In Figures 3-89 to 3-91, the planning and design of this residential street is isolated under the three components.

In Figure 3-89, the important characteristic is the alignment of the individual buildings so as to achieve a distinct spatial form and category—that is, a linear access space. As seen on the plan in Figure 3-88, the layout of the street itself has been provided with a bend at the midpoint, which reduces the scale of the space perceived at any position along the way. In functional terms, this discourages the rapid movement of cars while supporting more passive local use by pedestrians, bicycles, etc. Oriented east–west, the street space is defined by buildings that are lower on the south side so as to provide maximum exposure to the sun. (In very warm climates, this could be reversed.) Buildings are organized with varying heights and setbacks, which contribute to the more intimate scale and visual complexity while providing a wide variety of housing types.

Component Two

In Figure 3-90, openings are provided that are expressive, not only of various interior uses, but also of how these relate to the natural elements and to the public domain. In this connection, larger openings (balconies, etc.) are provided on the side facing the sun while various treatments at ground level provide zones of transition that are appropriate to the uses.

Component Three

In Figure 3-91, various ground treatments as well as furnishing are provided that are consistent with the character produced by Components One and Two. Traffic space is kept to a minimum while the use of trees, street lamps, seating, etc., all contribute to the varied use one would expect at this urban level.

COMPONENT 2

Figure 3-90.

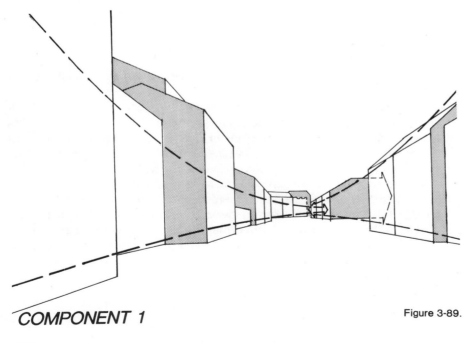

COMPONENT 1

Figure 3-89.

SECTION

COMPONENT 3

Figure 3-91.

CASE STUDY 2: A CITY CENTER

Our second study concerns the case of a typical central-city revitalization. A central shopping street of an average older city in the northeastern U.S.A., once an active commercial center, has gradually deteriorated as new shopping centers (malls) have been built in the more accessible outskirts. In this proposal, submitted by this writer in response to an R.F.P. (Request for Proposal), the three-component approach was applied within the context of an overall study of the city center.

In principle, it was suggested that the revitalization of the center required a comprehensive approach that extended beyond the question of making the central shopping street more supportive (Figure 3-93). In this connection, two basic structuring concepts were introduced. These two concepts, summarized in the plan in Figure 3-92, were that of (1) providing greater density in the matrix of linear spaces, and (2) introducing important new focal points and associated uses. With regard to the first of these two concepts, this involved the development of several new block-level pedestrian links that would give the center a more intense labyrinthlike quality. This would give the center a greater complexity and supportive quality without necessitating the closure of the central shopping street to traffic with all the associated problems this always entails. The treatment of the central shopping street would be limited to the elimination of much of the on-street parking, the widening of sidewalks, and the introduction of glass canopies, as in the Boston and Allentown examples seen earlier (Figures 2-137, 2-138). This would give the central shopping street added complexity and much-needed protection from the northern climate, while retaining its basic, multimodal access role in the city.

With regard to the second basic structuring concept, while a new river-front park was suggested to the north of the center (A in Figure 3-92) at the heart of the commercial area, a phased development for a new civic center was proposed (B in Figure 3-92). Built on a large city-owned parking lot (the vestiges of an earlier unsuccessful urban renewal effort), it would provide a combination of much-needed civic offices as well as commercial facilities, a municipal theater, and parking facilities (for which a government grant was on hand).

Ideally located within the access structure of the city center, this large site (Figure 3-95) could provide a new pole of attraction, not only in terms of the new uses introduced, but also in terms of providing a physical and spatial focus and crossroads at the city level. In this connection, a central characteristic of the proposal is a major new cluster space of the compound class. Well linked to the access system of the city, this cluster space would be given a clear and distinct form that would be supportive of many functions and activities.

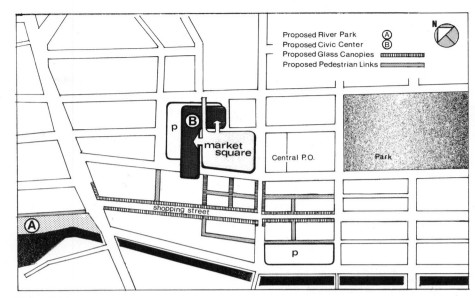

Figure 3-92.

Figure 3-93. Commercial street to be upgraded.

Component One

In the sketch in Figure 3-94, using the diagrammatic technique we introduced in Part Two (for structuring rather than analytic purposes), the principle of the new "bowllike" containing space is presented along with the use of a vertical focal element. Tying into existing and proposed access links, it provides a focal cluster space that could become the functional and symbolic heart of the city.

In the sketch in Figure 3-96, built forms associated with Component One are provided. Structure 1 includes a complex of civic offices on the upper levels while the ground level is given to active commercial uses. Structure 2, a municipal theater, because of its importance is given a somewhat independent form, while providing, in conjunction with structure 1 and an important existing building 3, a strong sense of spatial enclosure and definition to this northeastern corner of the new square. This would help to shield the space from the prevailing northeasterly winds and thus produce a supportive microclimate. The elevator tower at the center of structure 1 provides the square with a symbolic vertical feature. The sunken area in the southeast corner (4) is a large light and stairwell to provide clear linkage and continuity between the square and the lower-level parking area.

Figure 3-94.

COMPONENT 1 (diagram)

Figure 3-95. Site for proposed new market square.

205

Component Two

Under Component Two and in conjunction with a generalized program for these buildings, various treatments for window and door openings as well as for transition zones are suggested. In this connection, various degrees of permeability and interpenetration, which are expressive of the interrelationship of interior and exterior domains, is provided (Figure 3-97).

In the civic office building, a major opening provides a clear expression of entrance while establishing a high level of interpenetration between the public circulation space within the building and the square. As such it almost functions as an extension of the square into the building. At ground level, the zone of transition is placed within an arcade which also provides a high level of permeability. As can be seen, this building is extended in air-rights fashion over the existing sector-level street, thereby increasing the degree of definition and containment for the square while reducing the visual importance of the incoming linear space. The treatment for the area fronting the municipal theater provides a highly three-dimensional transition space that would ensure a permanent year-round center of activity for the square. The glass structure largely blurs the borders between interior and exterior domains. While smaller and appropriate window openings (not shown) would be developed in conjunction with specific program requirements, the western end of the civic office building, if used as a major public meeting space, for example, could be provided with a large window opening expressive of this function.

Component Three

Under Component Three, which is included in Figure 3-97, various ground treatments and furnishing are introduced. Changes of level help to delineate and separate access and activity areas while also providing sitting areas. While an elevated walkway similar to the one in Toronto (Figure 2-111,a,b), provides an added degree of spatial containment on the western side, the use of trees also contributes to this end. A pavilion structure at the southwestern end contributes to the subdivision of the space into a more complex shape while providing a location for a combined information center and restaurant. Various activities in the main space, like a weekly farmers' market, special events (associated with an existing summer festival), etc., could be facilitated with the use of various temporary structures. In wintertime, the cold climate would permit the use of a portion of the square for an ice-skating rink (where the market is shown), thus making this space a year-round permanent attraction. Various localized focal elements, a statue, a fountain, etc., further help to structure the space while seating, both fixed and movable, are also provided.

COMPONENT 1

Figure 3-96.

206

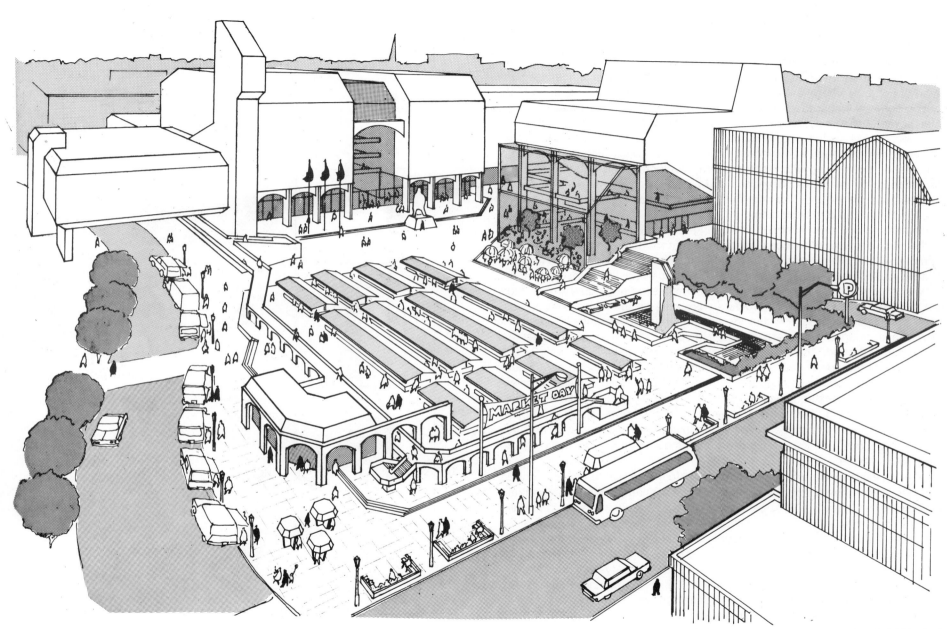

COMPONENT 2 and 3

Figure 3-97. Proposed new market square and civic center.

CASE STUDY 3: A COLLEGE CAMPUS

A college campus is in many ways a microcosm of the city. It incorporates a wide variety of facilities within a limited area, serving the needs of a distinct community on a day-to-day basis. Within such a dense and almost medieval type of context, where access is frequently pedestrian, the importance of the public domain of shared spaces, in terms of expressive and supportive qualities, is vital. Frequently, however, because campus planning and development has been heavily influenced by modern concepts of spaciousness, the sense of openness has been achieved at the expense of basic use questions. For this reason they share with many modern developments a strong lack of differentiation in their common spaces and a correspondingly low level of supportive capacity for use. Our third case study, a small college in New York, is a typical example of this situation.

Begun through the conversion of existing residential and industrial buildings in the early decades of this century, the present form and consolidation of this campus was largely associated with a major urban-renewal project in the early sixties. At this time several old residential buildings within the present campus, as well as in the surrounding blocks, were demolished and some streets were closed. New private residential towers were built on the newly cleared adjacent sites while the space within the campus was left essentially open. The new sense of spaciousness provided a much-needed break in the densely urban neighborhood. The result, however, as can be seen in Figures 3-99 to 3-102 is that the open space within the campus lacks the kind of spatial form quality that can sustain and support a variety of uses. Buildings are perceived as independent, freestanding forms while the rambling spaces between remain largely underutilized. Additional problems associated with this type of open-order development are those of security. Limited use and few eyes on these spaces produces a degree of insecurity that is both real and imagined, particularly at nighttime.

In an analysis of the campus in terms of built and spatial forms, it is instructive to consider the impact of the buildings by reversing the figure/ground relationship as in Figure 3-103. Here it becomes evident to what extent the buildings remain independent and unrelated to the public spaces. But for a few areas like A and B (Figure 3-103), spaces remain largely undifferentiated and do not 'speak of their functions' through their forms. The use of trees however, when they are in season, does contribute to spatial quality on the campus.

The major axis running east–west (C in Figure 3-103 and Figure 3-99), once a neighborhood street, is weak in definition and is not expressive of its present pedestrian role. Its scale and treatment speak of wheeled traffic and the pedestrian feels out of place. Though providing the major link with the surrounding street system, this axis has been largely duplicated by a path through

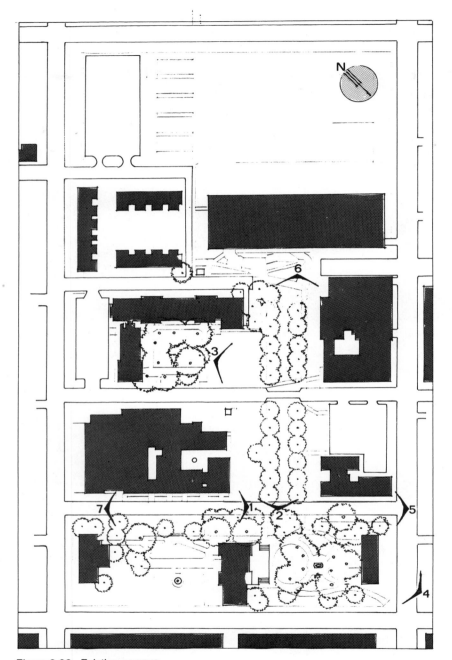

Figure 3-98. Existing campus

Figure 3-99. East-west axis (view 1 on plan Figure 3-98).

Figure 3-100. North-south axis (view 2 on plan, Figure 3-98).

Figure 3-101. North-south axis (view 3 on plan, Figure 3-98).

Figure 3-102. View 4 on plan Figure 3-98.

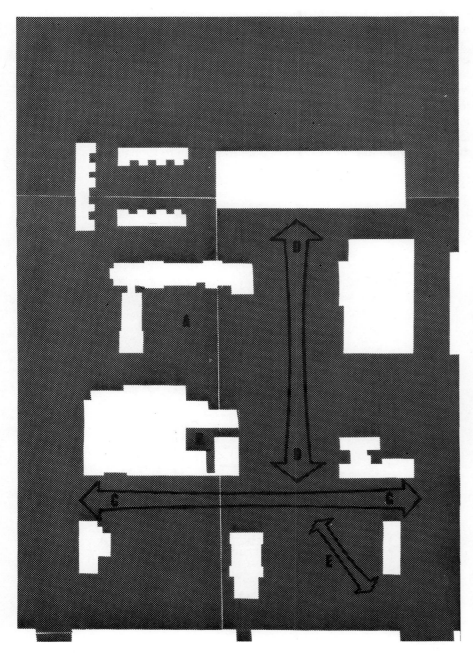

Figure 3-103. Figure-ground plan.

an otherwise passive space (Figure 3-104). The major north–south axis (D in Figure 3-103 and Figures 3-100, 3-101), a grass mall, is highly fragmented due to large gaps on either side while terminating on a fieldhouse which lacks both the scale and focal character needed to enclose the space. Though the character and axial function of this space is improved by trees, these have the limitation of being only ephemeral skeletons for the better part of the academic year.

The major objectives of this plan have been those of identifying and strengthening present access and use patterns by rationalizing existing conditions, while also introducing additional uses with new infill buildings. In the plan in Figure 3-105, the basic access and use functions that have generated the proposal are summarized. The emphasis has been on the reinforcement of the two cross-axes which form the basic organizational structure of the campus. This has also involved a minor relocation of the third axis (E) mentioned above.

Figure 3-104. Access link, E on plan 3-103.

In the plan in Figure 3-106, new academic (a), administrative (b), and student residence buildings (c), reflecting projected and potential medium to long-range developments for the college, are located within these structures, thus providing a variety of uses that would activate the major communal spaces of the campus and also reduce the security problem. While the junction of the main east–west axis with the surrounding streets has been affirmed, as can be seen in the sketch in Figure 3-108, the mall that comprises the main north–south axis has also been given clearer spatial definition (Figure 3-110). At the point of junction and crossing of the two axes at the center of the campus, a student center (d), and an extension of an existing student residence (e), form a new strategic cluster space or square (Figure 3-111). This space would act as a symbolic heart for the campus while also providing a distinct meeting space on campus. A bookstore and coffeehouse could be located at the ground level opening out out onto the square. As can be seen in this isometric, a highly ornate flagpole (relocated from a now inconspicuous position on campus) could provide a focal element in the center of the new square. This would reaffirm the role of this space as the central space on campus as well as the juncture of the two major axis which comprise the visual and access structure. At the end of the grass mall (D in Figure 3-103) a now disused but highly ornate stone entrance pavillion (formerly part of the library

but later removed) could be relocated (see sketch 3-110). This could provide a sence of historical continuity as well as a visual terminus to the mall which is now lacking. In the final sketch in Figure 3-113, the treatment of the main east–west axis in terms of ground materials, the use of small structures, and furnishing (Component Three) shows how this important access route can be made to express its pedestrian role while also providing supportive conditions for more intense, related uses on a day-to-day basis. The relocated route through the now more distinctly defined space (E mentioned earlier) has been formalized to reflect its intense use by students approaching the campus from the south, while the introduction of a gateway feature formalizes its role.

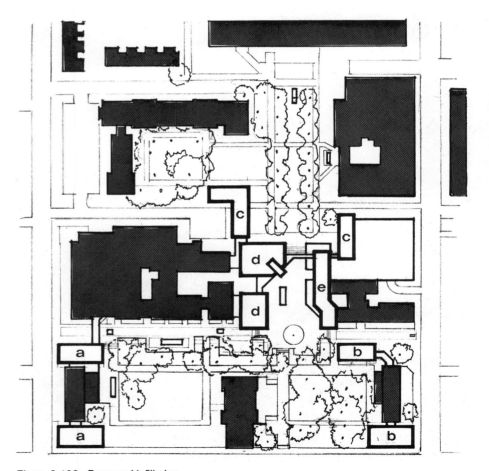

Figure 3-106. Proposed infill plan.

Figure 3-105. Basic campus organization and access system.

Figure 3-107. East-west axis entrance (view 5 on plan, Figure 3-98)

Figure 3-108. Proposed infill and treatment.

Figure 3-109. North-south axis. (view 6 on Figure 3-98).

Figure 3-110. Proposed infill and treatment.

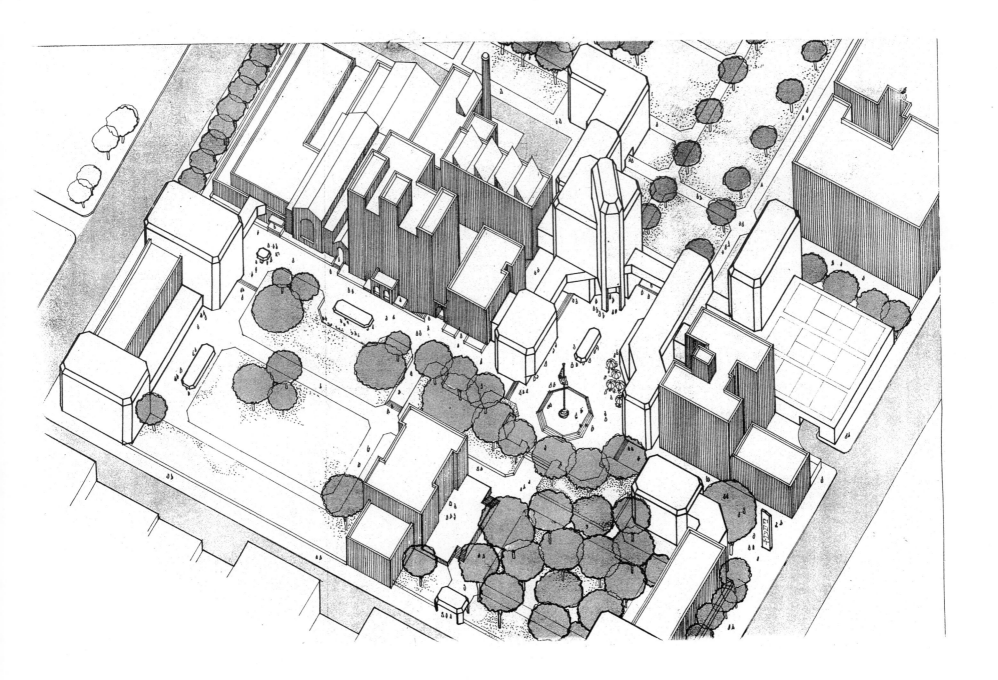

Figure 3-111. Proposed central square.

Figure 3-112. East-west axis (view 7 on Figure 3-98).

Figure 3-113. Proposed treatment.

CONCLUSION

In concluding this examination, we can ask the question with which we started: To what extent is the public domain relevant today? Modern society has become highly pluralistic, individualistic, and dispersed by comparison with all earlier eras. It would seem that the public domain, as a system of distinctly supportive spaces, speaks of another time when social coherence and human interaction were more important dimensions of the human experience.

And yet, basic and fundamental human needs for action and interaction, for intensity, creative involvement and identity with a reality beyond one's immediate private domain, persist. Within the highly diluted open order, the proliferation of "centers," commercial, athletic, cultural etc., are not only the product of convenience and enterprising entrepreneurship, but evidence of continuing human needs to communicate and participate within a social environment and context. In these increasingly complex centers, one finds a parody of what the traditional city has always offered, variety, surprise and identity with a larger social body. Increasingly, the operators of these centers have discovered that the more their centers resemble medieval towns in terms of variety, complexity and lots of places where people can just sit around, acting, observing, and just being human, the more they are successful. The wheel is being reinvented.

On the other hand, both the enormous revival of traditional city centers as well as the growing popularity of villagelike residential developments, demonstrates how the need and desire for more expressive and supportive conditions is now being felt in other areas. It has become increasingly clear, however, that the physical forms that provide a context for communities has only a limited impact on questions of social cohesion, interaction, etc. These are social, cultural, psychological, and political questions before they become physical. And yet, these are all intimately interrelated.

The challenge that lies ahead for planners and designers with regard to the built environment is to provide a better relationship between people and form. For this purpose the emphasis must be less on forms per se than on the implications of form in people's experience. This goes beyond the "appearance" of forms and concerns the impact they have in people's lives. No simple reversion to past forms will do, nor will the use of wild science-fiction solutions based on high-tech gadgets and imagery. The journey forward lies first through the inner regions of the human mind, where a great deal must be learned about what being truly human is all about. It is hoped that this book, though providing only a brief tour, has been of some assistance.

Figure 3-114. New Market, Philadelphia, Pennsylvania.

the human need for action and interaction persists

217

Notes and References—PART THREE

1. Again here it is important to stress that the critical question which this book is focussed on is use. In this connection the term use as suggested refers to a very wide variety of functions and activities, but the major emphasis is on making spaces appropriate and meaningful in people's daily lives. As such, uses will vary enormously depending on the specific context. In some cases a symbolic role, setting off major monuments like Notre Dame cathedral in Paris, will generate use. In that case, the gathering of tourist and occasional special functions will require fewer additional supports. The critical concern remains that of ensuring that a high level of coordination occur between design and planning choices with a specific understanding of the physical characteristics and supports which will be needed in order to ensure that the public spaces produced will not end up as dead spaces having neither functional nor symbolic roles.

   As mentioned in the text, the analysis of individual spaces, in order to be complete, relies on an intimate knowledge of the specific context involved. An understanding of their roles at various times of day, week, year (seasons), etc. is essential. In this connection, some of the spaces analysed in this section perform special events roles at certain times while remaining relatively idle at others. (See Kevin Lynch's *What Time is This Place,* MIT Press, Cambridge, 1972.) The appropriateness of such varying use can be valid but must be anticipated at the design/planning stage. A major concern is that of overspecializing and thus limiting the potential of spaces particularly where their locations are highly strategic.

   An example where this has been a problem is the Guild Hall square in Portsmouth England (Figure 1-68). Here what had formerly been a highly central and strategic square through which the city's major streets crossed has been turned into an essentially inverted and largely isolated space. No longer functioning as a crossroads its use is now limited to that of special events while remaining largely idle at other times. The lack of commercial activities within the new civic offices building which defines and encloses the space has further contributed to this restricted role. Its value to the city as an active heart has subsequently been reduced to that of a formal and symbolic ballroom which might have been more appropriately located in a less strategic location. It should be emphasized that total pedestrianization, though intellectually appealing, is not necessarily or always desirable nor a sure formula for success. Indeed, if not appropriate to the context, it can often be a formula for disuse.

2. It should be noted that the three case studies in this section in order to include each of the three components discussed in Part Two go well beyond what could be appropriately regulated through planning and design guidelines. This is particularly true with regards to component two, the treatment of facades. Here both the organization of surfaces as well as the choice and disposition of openings associated with specific programs is provided only for the purpose of demonstrating the principles discussed in the text.

   The development of planning-design guidelines is something which will vary enormously from one context to another. The basic concern here and throughout this book is that of emphasizing the importance of linking planning and design choices and decisions at an early stage in order that a meaningful and supportive urban environment can be produced.

3. In the development of hybrid solutions to urban streets, the degree of enclosure produced by buildings can be varied. In this case study, for example, the number of buildings directly adjoining the space could be reduced and replaced with other enclosing devices like fences, tall hedges, etc. without seriously compromising the sense of spatial enclosure.

4. This case study is a further development of a proposal which was submitted for the city of Lewiston in Maine. The development of the new civic center was in fact outside of the immediate study area and RFP, which were basically concerned with the treatment of the central street mentioned. As such the proposed center was essentially conceptual and represents the kind of planning and design opportunity and initiative that is often needed in order to provide both a structuring feature with which public interest and involvement (as well as private investment) can be more easily generated and mobilized. As such, it provided less a definitve and final static proposal than a catalyst for discussion and the basis for further study.

5. This case study at Pratt Institute in Brooklyn is based on student projects which were done within an urban design studio tutored by this writer. Based on the analysis of existing use patterns as well as extensive discussions with the college administration, the proposed infill buildings represent possible long-range development goals. One major aim of the study however, was that of investigating the development potential of the existing campus. As such it was to contribute to the development of a program rather than to merely siting a predetermined program. Along a similar line of investigation is the study by Christopher Alexandre, *The Oregon Experiment.* (Oxford University Press, New York, 1975)

   Much gratitude is offered to the administration of Pratt Institute for their support and willing cooperation in this study.

INDEX

SUBJECT
TO RECALL **DATE DUE**

Demco, Inc. 38-293